Self-Care For Morticians

Elena Blackwood

Published by Defenestration Press, 2024.

SELF-CARE FOR MORTICIANS

First edition. February 10, 2024.

ISBN: 979-8224384075

Written by Elena Blackwood.

Table of Contents

To all the compassionate souls in the field of deathcare, whose unwavering dedication to serving others often comes at the expense of their own well-being.

This book is dedicated to you—the morticians, funeral directors, embalmers, and caregivers—who tirelessly tend to the needs of the departed and offer solace to the grieving.

May these pages serve as a beacon of light in your darkest hours, a reminder to nurture yourselves with the same compassion and care you extend to others.

Your commitment to dignity, reverence, and compassion inspires us all. Thank you for your invaluable service to humanity.

With profound gratitude,

Elena Blackwood

Introduction

The Call of Mortuary

I held the receiver to my ear, and on the other end, a voice, fragile and full of grief, trembled. They were lost, unsure of where to turn, seeking guidance on how to handle the sudden loss of a loved one. My heart swelled with empathy, and I felt a deep sense of urgency to help ease their burden.

Death had always intrigued me, growing up. My parents, who owned a funeral home, instilled in me a reverence for the rituals and traditions that accompany the final moments of a person's life. While my friends played sports and rode bikes, I found solace in books about mortuary practices, and even attended funerals with my parents.

As I grew older, my curiosity about mortality only intensified. I delved into the history and cultural significance of death rituals, exploring everything from ancient Egyptian embalming to modern-day cremation. Fuelled by this fascination and my desire to help others, I knew I had found my calling in mortuary care.

After completing my training as a mortician, I eagerly joined my parents' funeral home. It became natural for me to embalm bodies, console grieving families, and coordinate funeral arrangements. It was a difficult job, but one I was compelled to do.

But over time, the weight of the work began to take its toll. The constant exposure to death and grief wore me down, chipping away at my emotional well-being. I grew weary and overwhelmed, struggling to find solace in the midst of so much loss. It was then that I knew I needed to prioritize self-care, so that I could continue providing the support and compassion families relied on me for.

I started carving out moments in my day for quiet reflection, embracing the stillness amidst the chaos. Whether it was a few minutes of meditation or a walk in nature, these moments nourished my emotional needs, recharging my energy, and strengthening my resilience.

I sought support from my colleagues and peers in the mortuary field, meeting regularly to share our experiences, struggles, and triumphs. Together, we formed a close-knit community that understood and encouraged one another in times of difficulty. Through these connections, I discovered that I wasn't alone in my struggles. Self-care wasn't a luxury, but a necessity for all of us in our profession.

In my research, I uncovered various techniques and practices that could help morticians cope with stress and compassion fatigue. From engaging in physical activities like yoga and exercise to exploring creative outlets such as writing or painting, I found comfort in journaling, allowing my emotions to spill onto the pages, granting me release and clarity.

Taking breaks from the funeral home environment also became essential. Stepping away from the constant reminders of mortality allowed me to recharge and find balance. Whether it was a weekend getaway or spending quality time with loved ones, these breaks reminded me of the beauty and joy that still existed in life, even in the face of death.

Self-care also meant setting boundaries and learning to say no when necessary. While our work is centered on serving others, it's important to recognize our limitations and prioritize our own well-being. It could be challenging, especially when faced with families in desperate need of assistance, but finding that balance between caring for others and caring for ourselves was crucial for our long-term sustainability.

Throughout my journey of self-care and reflection, I've come to appreciate the immense importance of our profession. Morticians aren't merely caretakers of the deceased; we are healers, champions of compassion, and guides on the path to closure. We hold the sacred responsibility of providing support and solace to grieving families during their darkest moments.

I aspire to guide all those in the mortuary profession. By sharing my experiences and research, I hope to empower my fellow morticians to prioritize their own well-being, so that they can continue to offer the utmost care and compassion to those who seek their guidance.

That life-changing call set me on a path of immense growth and self-discovery. Through the ups and downs, the tears and the laughter, I found purpose in helping others navigate the intricate terrain of grief. And as I recount my journey in these pages, may it serve as a reminder that even in the face of death, self-care and compassion are the pillars on which we build our strength.

The Dark Side of Compassion

I FEEL AS THOUGH I am preaching to the choir, but, as a mortician, let me tell you, death and loss are no strangers to us. I mean, it's our daily grind. We're the ones who handle the bodies of the deceased, comfort grieving families, and make sure their loved ones get the dignified farewell they deserve. It's not for the faint of heart, that's for sure. We bear witness to the rawest, most real flood of emotions from those who are left behind. Their pain becomes our pain, you know? It's like we take on their sorrow and carry it with us long after we've left the funeral home. And let me tell you, it takes a toll on us.

Picture this: darkness closing in around you, smothering you like a heavy blanket. And I don't just mean emotionally - this stuff weighs on you physically, too. The intense emotions we encounter every single day can seep into our souls, leaving us feeling drained and empty. It's like we absorb all the pain and sorrow of those we serve, and it lingers with us long after the mourners have gone. This job doesn't just mess with our heads and hearts, it messes with our whole well-being.

Folks like us, constantly exposed to the grief of others, have higher stress, anxiety, and depression levels. And guess what? We're also more likely to suffer from compassion fatigue. That's when you're so emotionally wiped out that you become cynical, detached, and have trouble empathizing with others. Sounds like a jolly ol' time, right?

Let me tell you, those findings hit me like a ton of bricks. I've seen firsthand how carrying the weight of compassion can become unbearable. The faces of my clients, etched with the deepest grief, follow me into my dreams. Their tears echo in my mind, long after they've dried. Their pain, it becomes my burden, my cross to bear.

And it's not just one loss that gets to us, it's the accumulation of years immersed in the darkest moments of others' lives. Each new loss piles up on top of the last, until we're like sponges saturated with sorrow, unable to wring ourselves out. It's suffocating, really. And I'm sure each of you, if I were to ask you to name which family you've worked with, which undertaking you have worked on, which of those are the ones that have stuck with you for however many years, I'm sure many of you will be able to tell me more than one.

But you know what makes it even harder? The expectations thrust upon us. We're supposed to be these strong, unflinching figures, always providing support and stability to those in need. There is no room for our vulnerability. We have to be their rocks, even when we're crumbling inside. And let me tell you, that pressure combined with the emotional toll of our work can leave us feeling isolated and all alone in our struggles.

In those moments of quiet reflection, I find myself wondering if all this pain and sacrifice is a necessary part of the job. Can we find a way to keep our compassion alive without losing ourselves in the process? Is there some kind of balance we can strike?

You know, I don't have the answers to those questions just yet. But what I do know is that acknowledging the dark side of compassion is the first step towards finding that balance. We have to recognize that our empathy and understanding, as beautiful and powerful as they are, can also become overwhelming burdens. We have to prioritize our own well-being, set boundaries to make sure we don't drown in the pain of others.

Now, I won't lie to you, this journey towards self-care isn't going to be a walk in the park. It requires us to face our own vulnerabilities, to admit that we, too, need support and solace. We have to make time to process our own emotions, seek help when we need it, and surround ourselves with understanding and compassionate people who've got our backs.

In the chapters ahead, I'm going to dive into different strategies and techniques that can help us morticians cope with the dark side of compassion. We need tools like mindfulness practices and boundary-setting to protect ourselves from emotional exhaustion and build up our resilience. We have to learn how to take care of ourselves so we can continue to offer solace and support to those who need it, without losing ourselves in the process.

My hope for this book is that it becomes a guide for my fellow morticians, a compass to help us navigate those treacherous waters of compassion fatigue. We're the caregivers, healers, and guides through the human experience. Our work matters, but so does our own well-being. By putting self-care at the top of our priority list and learning how to handle the dark side of compassion, we can keep doing what we do best: soothing souls and providing comfort in times of need.

The Masks We Wear

DEATH IS ALWAYS LOOMING over us, like a thick fog that refuses to lift. It's a constant presence in our lives, a force that we, as caretakers of the deceased, are all too familiar with. We have a responsibility to handle the departed with care, to prepare them for their final goodbyes, and to offer comfort to grieving families. We strive to be the pillar of strength for those who desperately need it. But what happens when we, the ones who handle death on a daily basis, need someone to lean on?

When I step into the funeral home, I transform into a picture of calmness, a beacon of professionalism even in the face of unimaginable loss. It's like I'm putting on a mask, tucking away my own grief and anxieties in a hidden compartment of my mind. The weight of the world settles on my shoulders, but somehow, I carry it with grace and ease.

But this constant strength, this façade of invulnerability, takes its toll. It's exhausting to always wear a mask, to suppress the very emotions that make us human. Our job demands that we be reserved, that we keep our feelings locked away, and in the process, we lose a part of ourselves.

As days turn into weeks, and weeks turn into months and years, the masks become a part of who we are. They become ingrained in our identity, and we start to forget who we truly are. We morph into stoic figures, with our emotions hidden deep within the recesses of our hearts.

But those emotions don't disappear. They linger, haunting us in those quiet moments when we're left alone with our thoughts. They seep into our dreams, turning them into twisted nightmares. They chip away at our mental and emotional wellbeing, wearing down the resilience we once had.

Compassion fatigue sets in, an emotional exhaustion that comes from constantly being exposed to trauma and suffering. We become numb to the pain, desensitized to the sorrow that surrounds us. It's like we're standing on the edge of a precipice, our own emotions threatening to push us over.

And yet, despite the toll it takes on us, we keep wearing these masks. We keep hiding our vulnerability, afraid that showing our true selves will be seen as weakness. We worry that revealing our pain will undermine the trust and faith that families place in us during their darkest moments.

But it's crucial that we break free from this cycle of masking our true emotions. We need to acknowledge and embrace our vulnerability because that's how true healing begins. Our strength doesn't lie in suppressing our emotions, but in confronting and addressing our own pain.

We must prioritize self-care for our own wellbeing. We need to carve out moments of respite, moments to step away from the funeral home and tend to our own emotional needs. It could be engaging in a hobby, seeking therapy, or finding solace in the warm embrace of loved ones who understand the weight we carry.

By taking off the masks we wear, we can start building ourselves back up. We can find the strength to be both caretakers and individuals, honoring our own emotional needs while providing solace to those who are grieving. Through this act of self-care, we reclaim our humanity, and in doing so, we become even better at our role as morticians.

The masks we wear as morticians serve a purpose. They offer a semblance of strength and stability in the face of death. But at the same time, these masks come at a cost. They wear us down and erode our own wellbeing. It's vital that we acknowledge and embrace our vulnerability, allowing ourselves to heal and seek self-care. By peeling back the layers and revealing our true selves, we can not only survive but thrive as compassionate and resilient caretakers of the dead.

The Dance With Death

COME ON IN AND TAKE a step into my world. I want to share with you the ups and downs, the moments of sorrow, reflection, and the delicate balance between detachment and empathy that I experience in the mortuary profession. It's not always easy, but it's certainly fascinating.

Let's start at the beginning of this dance. When a loved one arrives at the funeral home, it's like a heavy cloud descends upon the place. They carry their grief like a burden and it's our job to be there for them, offering solace and support. We become their confidants, their rocks when their world is falling apart.

And as this dance continues, we dive headfirst into the practical aspects of our work. We meticulously prepare the bodies, dressing them up in their Sunday best, making them look peaceful and at rest. It's a point of pride for us to give the deceased back their dignity and present them to their loved ones in a way that brings peace and closure.

But let me tell you, underneath the surface of this dance lies a deeper journey. It's a journey that takes us to the depths of our own emotions. We're face to face with death daily and it's a constant reminder of our own mortality. The fragility of life lurks around every corner, whispering in our ears. We're trying to navigate our own existence while surrounded by reminders of our own inevitable departure.

In those moments of solitude, when the funeral home is empty and the silence engulfs us, we reflect on our own lives.

We think about the choices we've made and the impact we've had on those around us. The weight of our responsibility sits heavy on our shoulders, pushing us to find meaning in this fleeting life.

As morticians, we walk a fine line between detachment and empathy. We have to remain composed and professional, but at the same time, offer a compassionate presence to those who are grieving. We witness unimaginable pain, the raw outpouring of loss. And in those moments, we dig deep and find the empathy within us to listen and offer a soothing touch.

But here's the thing, this dance also requires us to be on guard against compassion fatigue. The continuous exposure to sorrow and loss can wear us down. We have to recognize the signs of burnout and fatigue and take care of ourselves. Self-care becomes crucial in this line of work.

For me, this dance with death has become a testament to the fragility of life and the resilience of the human spirit. It's taught me to cherish every single moment, to find beauty in the face of death. It's given me a profound understanding of how connected we all are in our experiences of grief and loss.

By sharing these intimate details of my dance with death, my hope is to offer insight and support to my fellow morticians. We play an essential role in the grieving process, entrusted with the sacred duty of honoring those who have passed. But amidst all the challenges and complexities, we must never forget to care for ourselves.

This dance is a dance of compassion, of resilience, and of self-discovery. It shapes us, challenges us, and ultimately makes us stronger. Through this dance, we find purpose and meaning as we hold space for both the departed and the grieving. It reminds us of the beauty of life, even in the face of death.

The Power of Self-Care

AS I DIVE INTO THE topic of self-care in the mortuary profession, I can't help but reflect on my own journey and the struggles I faced in my early days. Like so many of my colleagues, I entered this profession because of my immense compassion and desire to support others during their most vulnerable moments. But it didn't take long for me to realize that the demands of the job were taking a toll on my own emotional and mental well-being.

Let me tell you, being a mortician is no walk in the park. We work long hours, often doing physically demanding tasks. And let's not forget about the emotional weight we carry on our shoulders. We're constantly faced with the raw emotions of grieving families, and it can be incredibly challenging to process and hold the weight of their pain day in and day out. Compassion fatigue? Oh, you better believe it became my new (and unwelcome) reality. I found myself drained and struggling to find meaning and fulfillment in my work.

So, in my desperate search for answers, I began to explore the power of self-care. How could I restore the spark that had initially drawn me to this profession? How could I find balance amidst the chaos? One of the first tools I stumbled upon was mindfulness. Have you heard of it? It's this practice that asks us to be fully present, accepting ourselves without judgment, and letting go of distractions and worries. Let me tell you, it works wonders. Through mindfulness exercises, I learned to find a sense of calm even in the midst of chaos. It helped me stay grounded, allowing me to be fully present for the families I served, while still honoring my own emotional needs.

But that's not all I found. Oh no, there was so much more. I discovered the incredible power of creative expression. See, in our line of work, we come face to face with the deeply emotional and often tragic stories of those we serve. And boy, can those stories weigh heavy on our hearts. So, I started writing. I poured my thoughts and feelings onto the pages of my journal, revealing my pain and my triumphs. It was like therapy, giving me a release and a way to honor the experiences of those I encountered.

And let's not forget about physical self-care, my friend. Our bodies go through it all in this job. So, taking care of myself physically became a top priority. Whether it was a jog in the park or a yoga class, getting my body moving released so much tension and boosted my energy. And let me tell you, I made sleep and relaxation a non-negotiable. The demanding nature of our work leaves us drained, physically and emotionally. So, creating a peaceful sleep environment and establishing a nighttime routine made all the difference. I woke up feeling ready to conquer the day, and that's a feeling worth its weight in gold.

I realized self-care went beyond just managing stress and burnout. It was about finding joy and fulfillment in my personal life too. It was about prioritizing the activities and relationships that brought me happiness and nourished my soul. So, I made time for loved ones, indulged in my hobbies, and carved out moments just for me. Self-care wasn't something I only practiced within the walls of the mortuary—it encompassed every aspect of my being.

Here's the thing, my friend. This profession can be tough. It's emotionally taxing and can leave you feeling overwhelmed. But at the same time, there's something beautiful about it. It offers growth, compassion, and undeniable connection. And that's why self-care is a necessity, not a luxury, for us morticians. We owe it to ourselves and to the families we serve to prioritize our well-being and find a sense of balance within the demands of our work.

From mindfulness exercises to creative outlets, I'll share practical tools and strategies that have helped me navigate the challenges of this rewarding yet demanding profession. My hope is that by sharing my own insights, I can empower my fellow morticians to prioritize their self-care and find resilience and fulfillment in their work. Self-care isn't selfish—it's an act of compassion, for ourselves and for those who rely on us during their most vulnerable moments. So, let's embark on this journey together as we explore the power of self-care in the mortuary profession. Are you ready?

Welcome to the World of Mortuary Science

A Glimpse Into the Unknown

As I stepped into the hallowed hallways of the mortuary, it felt as though the walls themselves were whispering the secrets of those who lay at rest within. The air was heavy with the lingering scent of embalming chemicals, a constant reminder of the solemnity that permeated every corner of this place. It's a strange thing, you know, to work with the deceased day in and day out. But as I walked through those corridors, I couldn't help but feel a deep sense of connection to the past, to a time when death was not the taboo subject it is today.

In the days of old, families would gather around their departed loved ones, washing their bodies, preparing them for a final farewell. Death was not hidden away, but rather embraced as a natural part of the cycle of life. The mortuary, with its long-standing traditions and reverence, was at the heart of it all. But somewhere along the way, we, as a society, lost touch with death. We began to distance ourselves from its inevitable embrace, turning it into something to be feared, something to be avoided.

And so, the mortuary became a place shrouded in mystery, hidden away from public view. Death became a subject too uncomfortable to discuss, too morbid to even think about. But I believe that this distance from death has led to a disconnection from our own humanity. We have become unfamiliar with the depths of grief, unprepared to face our own mortality or cope with the loss of those we hold dear. And that is where the mortician comes in.

The world of mortuary science is one that both fascinates and repels. It requires a delicate balance between technical expertise and emotional resilience. As a mortician, I am tasked not only with the practical aspects of preparing the deceased for their eternal slumber but also with providing comfort and support to those left behind. It is a profession that demands unwavering compassion and professionalism, a calling that holds within it profound responsibilities.

As I submerged myself in the study of mortuary science, I began to uncover the rich tapestry of history and culture that surrounds death and funerary rituals. From the ancient civilizations practicing the art of mummification to the elaborate Victorian customs of mourning, death has always played a pivotal role in the fabric of human society. The more I learned, the more I realized the importance of acknowledging and embracing death as an integral part of life's journey. It was through this understanding that I found the strength to face the challenges that lay ahead.

One of the greatest challenges in the realm of mortuary science is the toll it takes on our emotional well-being. The constant exposure to death and grief can slowly chip away at one's soul, leaving us feeling drained and detached. It's what they call compassion fatigue, a term often used in the healthcare field. But we morticians are not exempt from this phenomenon. That's why self-care becomes paramount, a lifeline that keeps us afloat amidst the turbulent waters of our profession.

In my quest to find ways to not only survive but thrive in this demanding field, I discovered an array of strategies to combat stress and compassion fatigue. Taking a moment for meditation, for grounding ourselves in the present, allows our minds to find respite from the daily grind. Seeking support from fellow morticians, finding solace in the shared experiences of our colleagues, creates a safe haven where our emotions can be laid bare. And of course, nurturing our own lives outside of work, tending to our passions and maintaining a healthy work-life balance, all contribute to our overall well-being.

Through my own experiences and the stories shared with me by fellow morticians, I have witnessed the transformative power of self-care. By prioritizing our own mental and emotional health, we not only preserve our own sanity but also enhance the care we provide to those who need it most. Being able to navigate the depths of grief and loss with compassion and empathy is a testament to the resilience and dedication we bring to this profession.

So, as we journey deeper into the realms of mortuary science together, I invite you to embrace the unknown with me. In the chapters that lie ahead, we will explore the intricacies of embalming, preservation, and the spiritual significance of funerary rituals. We will peel back the layers, confront the myths, and unravel the mysteries that have long surrounded our profession. And most importantly, we will uncover the self-care strategies that can sustain us in the face of the most challenging of times. So, my friend, let us embark on this extraordinary journey hand in hand and discover the beauty that lies within the realm of mortuary science.

The Anatomy of Death

YOU KNOW, AS MORTICIANS, we're no strangers to death. The whole process of watching someone go from living to, well, whatever comes next, it's something we've seen time and time again. And it's our job to guide the departed and their loved ones through this whole ordeal with care and professionalism. We're like the tour guides of the afterlife, if you will.

And let me tell you, death ain't no walk in the park. Autopsies, in particular, are like the holy grail of forensic science. They help us unravel the mysteries surrounding a person's death. It's like a macabre treasure hunt, trying to find that one clue that'll solve the puzzle. It's strange though, you know? Our bodies are these incredible works of art, keeping us alive and kicking. But once we're gone, those once vital organs become nothing more than faded memories of a dance they used to perform.

Autopsies aren't just about figuring out how a person died, though. It's a chance to witness the miracles of human anatomy. Every cut, every examination, it's like peeling back layers of a story that's tattooed on our bodies. And let me tell you, it's not just about science. It's an art form in itself. The precision of the dissection, the painting-like preservation of the body – it's like delicate brushstrokes on a canvas. We're scientists, yes, but there's also a sense of reverence for the dead that we bring to the table.

But let me tell you, autopsies are just the tip of the iceberg. Beyond that lies the world of embalming. Oh boy, embalming is a whole different ball game. It's a process that requires a delicate mix of technical expertise and scientific know-how. Injecting embalming fluid into the veins, preserving the dignity of the body – it's a task that demands both precision and care. It's like we're dancing with chemicals, trying to find that perfect balance between rigidity and decay. You see, the goal isn't just to preserve the body, but to make sure it looks as dignified and graceful as the person did in life. We do so much work to make a person look great, even if that work will only be viewed for a few hours and then sealed up in a vault six feet underground or cremated. We do the best we can to give the family the goodbye they need.

Of course, we can't ignore the fact that, sooner or later, decomposition will come knocking. It's a fascinating and creepy transformation that we can't help but be intrigued by. The once vibrant skin turns pale and dull, almost like it forgot about the color wheel. The flesh softens, making it a playground for all those microscopic organisms that surround us. And slowly, the body goes back to where it came from, becoming one with the very earth it once walked on. It's a cycle, you know. It's death, but in its own weird way, it's life too.

For us morticians, decomposition serves as a sobering reminder that life is fleeting. It keeps us humble. We all come from the earth, and in the end, we'll all return to it. But you know, even in the midst of decay, there's something poetic about it. Those funky patterns formed by organisms, the intricate webs of fungi – they're not just about tearing us apart. They're proof that life and death are in this constant dance, intertwined, in this never-ending cycle.

So as we navigate the world of death, we have to approach it with both our brains and our hearts. These lifeless bodies we encounter, they were vessels, but they were filled with stories, memories, and emotions. And it's our duty to treat them with the respect they deserve, to give some comfort to those left behind.

The Dance of Emotions

BEING A MORTICIAN HAS opened my eyes to a whole new world of emotions. It all started with the first time I walked into a room filled with grieving families. Oh boy, the weight of loss was etched on their faces, like a heavy cloud hanging over them. It broke my heart to witness their sorrow and pain, as if I could feel it seeping into my own soul.

Each person had their own unique story, memories and emotions all intertwined with their grief. And let me tell you, their tears became like a glue that bonded their souls to mine. It was like we were in this together, going through the darkest of times. The compassion I had for them was both a blessing and a curse.

On one hand, compassion allowed me to really understand the magnitude of their pain. I could hold their hands and offer comfort when they needed it the most. But on the other hand, it exposed me to a whirlwind of emotions that threatened to consume me. Being compassionate requires vulnerability, and in this line of work, vulnerability is like walking on a tightrope.

In my mind, their loved one was nothing more than a body on my slab as I tried to work my magic to make them presentable after a horrendous car accident with nothing more than a few photographs to use as a map. When I speak with, or hear stories, of their loved one, that body becomes more real to me, it becomes a person who once had thoughts, dreams, and hopes, that all of a sudden came to an end, like a television show cancelled on a cliffhanger finale.

Watching families say their final goodbyes to their loved ones was a sight to behold. The sheer power of the human spirit was both heart-wrenching and awe-inspiring. The raw grief that emanated from them was so real and intense. It made me realize the incredible dance of emotions that morticians are privileged to witness.

We become the conduits for grief, allowing it to flow through us. We absorb some of the pain while providing a safe haven for healing. It's a delicate balance, like walking on a tightrope above a raging river. But it's also a beautiful dance, where we embrace the fragility of life and find beauty in the most unexpected places.

But being a mortician isn't just about witnessing grief. We also have the responsibility of preparing the body for its final resting place. It's a dance of reverence, precision, and artistry. Every stitch, every brush stroke is done with utmost care and understanding of both the physical and emotional aspects of death. It's a dance that reminds us of the fragility and beauty of life.

To navigate this emotional dance, I had to learn the art of detachment. It wasn't easy, let me tell you. There were moments when the weight of sorrow felt like it would swallow me whole. The memories of those I had cared for lingered on, etching themselves on my heart. But self-care became my lifeline.

I had to find solace in nature, take time to journal and release all those pent-up emotions, and seek support from my fellow morticians. Self-care became my compass in this emotional labyrinth. It taught me the importance of honoring my own emotions and acknowledging the toll this profession takes on my own well-being.

Through this dance of emotions, I discovered a strength and resilience I didn't know I had. It's a rollercoaster ride of compassion fatigue, where we give so much of ourselves but also need to replenish our emotional reserves. It's a delicate balance, and we can't do it alone.

Behind the somber silence of the mortuary, the dance of emotions continues. It's a beautiful tapestry woven with grief, compassion, and resilience. As morticians, we navigate this rollercoaster while holding hands with those who grieve, but we also have to protect our own hearts.

So take a deep breath, my fellow morticians, and let's continue this journey towards self-care in the world we live in.

The Weight of Responsibility

YOU KNOW, BEING A MORTICIAN is no easy gig. It comes with a hefty load of responsibility that can make your heart sink and your mind race. Every single day, I have to face the challenge of taking care of the dead, showing them the respect they deserve, and being there for their grieving families. Let me tell you, it's not a job for the faint of heart.

One of the toughest dilemmas we morticians face is figuring out how to honor the final wishes of the deceased. Sometimes they've left clear instructions for their send-off, but other times it's up to the family to make those tough decisions. It's like walking on a tightrope, trying to balance the dead's desires with what their loved ones want. It takes an incredible amount of empathy, open communication, and a deep respect for everyone involved.

And let's not forget about the law. As morticians, we're bound by regulations and laws that keep us on our toes. Hazardous materials? Check. Accurate records? Check.

Confidentiality? You bet. We always have to be on top of our game to make sure we stay on the right side of the law.

But it's not just about the deceased. We carry the weight of the grieving loved ones too. It's a delicate dance, providing comfort and support while still keeping our professional boundaries intact. We have to create a safe space for the grieving to let it all out, offer advice on funeral options, and connect them with counseling or support groups. It's like being a shoulder to cry on and a guide at the same damn time. Talk about multitasking.

From what I've seen, the backbone of being a mortician is built on empathy, compassion, and a fierce sense of duty. We know that what we do is essential to help the bereaved find closure and heal. Trust me, we don't take that responsibility lightly.

But you know what? We morticians can't do it all without taking care of ourselves. Self-care is a damn necessity in this field. We have to make sure our physical, emotional, and mental well-being are in tip-top shape so we can be fully present for the dead and their loved ones. That might mean getting some therapy or counseling to deal with the emotional rollercoaster, hitting the gym to fight off exhaustion, or finding moments of peace through mindfulness and meditation. Hey, we deserve a little peace among the chaos, right?

And here's the kicker - a solid support network is absolutely key. We need to connect with fellow morticians who get the unique challenges of this line of work, and we need to lean on our friends and family who offer love and support outside the embalming room. It's having those connections that make us feel like we're not alone in this battle.

So, to sum it all up, being a mortician is no joke. The responsibility we carry is immense, and it can feel like a ton of bricks on our shoulders. But with careful navigation of ethical dilemmas, following the laws to a T, and finding that delicate balance between our own well-being and our duty, we can keep doing this vital work with compassion and integrity. It's a tough gig, but someone's gotta do it.

The Forgotten Heroes

WHEN I THINK ABOUT death, I imagine more than just the final moments and the grieving loved ones. I think about the unsung heroes who work behind the scenes, ensuring that the departed are treated with the utmost dignity and respect. These morticians, often unnoticed and underappreciated, are the unsung heroes of the mortuary world, quietly carrying out their sacred duty.

Picture this: a mortician in a room, meticulously preparing a body for a funeral. The atmosphere is eerie, yet serene, like a sanctuary. The mortician, dressed in a crisp white lab coat, moves with purpose and care. Every action is a step towards restoring the deceased to a state of peaceful repose, offering solace to the grieving.

In the realm of the mortuary, time seems to stand still. The work of a mortician is intricate and precise. Every detail matters, from the positioning of the body to the delicate application of cosmetics. Years of education and experience have honed their skills, turning this space into a place of healing.

But it's not just technical expertise that makes a mortician special. They possess a resilience that is unmatched. They are intimately familiar with the harsh reality of death, witnessing its profound impact on both the living and the departed. They navigate the delicate balance between grief and professionalism, silently grieving themselves while providing solace to the bereaved.

As I delved deeper into the lives of morticians, I realized the sacrifices they make. Their profession demands long hours, often disregarding weekends and holidays. While the rest of the world takes time off, morticians stand ready to answer the calls of those in need, offering comfort and guidance to grieving families.

Yet, their work often goes unnoticed and underappreciated, overshadowed by more glamorous professions. But morticians find fulfillment in knowing that they have cared for someone who will never be able to say thank you. It is this selflessness that propels them forward, dedicating their lives to helping the grieving during their most vulnerable moments.

One of the biggest challenges that morticians face is dealing with compassion fatigue. Day after day, they bear the weight of grief, providing unwavering support to those in mourning. The sorrow of others becomes intertwined with their own, leaving a lasting mark on their hearts and minds. But morticians find ways to care for themselves, to preserve their emotional wellbeing.

I spoke with a mortician who shared her coping strategies, one of which was a daily meditation practice. Through this ritual, she found solace in the present moment, acknowledging her own emotions and releasing those she had absorbed from others. Mindful reflection became her refuge, a way to recover from the emotional toll of her work.

The mortuary world remains shrouded in silence, rarely brought to the forefront of public consciousness. The stories of these unsung heroes remain untold, hidden behind their composed and stoic exteriors. They are the quiet champions, the ones who offer solace in the face of loss, ensuring that the departed are honored with care and respect.

So, let's take a moment to honor and celebrate these forgotten heroes. They operate in the shadows, their work hidden from public view. Yet, they are the ones who witness the final moments, who bring comfort to the bereaved, and who uphold the sanctity of the mortuary. Let us extend our gratitude and reverence to these unsung heroes, for their dedication, compassion, and unwavering commitment to the final journeys of those who have departed.

Compassion in Crisis: The Role of Morticians

The Weight of Compassion

I've seen it all. I've seen the tears streaming down faces, the pain etched in every line, and the weight of grief that could crush a soul. Yeah, being a mortician is no walk in the park. My job is to be a pillar of strength, a rock for those who are drowning in their sorrow. And let me tell you, it's no easy task.

When families come to me, hearts heavy with loss, I have to set aside my own emotions and be there for them. I become a safe haven, a comforting presence in their darkest hours. But let me tell you, it's not as simple as it sounds. Their pain becomes mine, their grief seeping into my very being. It's a blessing and a curse, this ability to truly feel their suffering. I can't walk through a cemetary without being reminded of my work sitting just below the surface of the tombstones. The mangled bodies and crying families all come flooding back to me, and with each passing year, the cacophony the cemetery brings gets louder as more voices join the choir.

But here's the thing - carrying their burden takes a toll on my own well-being. It's like a constant weight on my chest, a sadness that lingers long after they've left my care. Day in and day out, I'm faced with death and loss. It wears on you, you know? It chips away at your resilience, leaving you feeling helpless and hopeless. It becomes hard to distinguish between who I am as a person and who I am as a mortician.

I've learned that the first step in dealing with this emotional load is acknowledging it. We morticians are not immune, despite what people may think. We're human, with our own needs and vulnerabilities. And it's crucial that we take care of ourselves if we want to continue providing compassionate care. Pushing our own emotions aside will only lead to burnout and exhaustion.

So, self-care becomes a lifeline. We have to be proactive in looking after ourselves, physically and emotionally. That could mean setting boundaries at work, creating a sacred space for reflection, or reaching out to colleagues or therapists for support. It's not selfish; it's necessary. By taking care of ourselves, we can keep showing up for the families who need us the most.

For me, carving out time every day for self-reflection has been a game-changer. Starting my morning with meditation and journaling grounds me before I step into the emotionally charged funeral home. It's my way of processing my own emotions and priming myself to be there for others.

And let me tell you, finding healthy outlets for stress and emotions is a must. Whether it's hitting the yoga mat, lacing up my running shoes, or just finding joy in a hobby, it all makes a difference. We need to nourish our souls outside of work, surround ourselves with loved ones, and soak in the healing power of nature.

But perhaps the most valuable support comes from our fellow morticians. They get it, you know? They understand the weight we carry, because they carry it too. Connecting with them can provide a sense of camaraderie, validation, and wisdom. It's a reminder that we're not alone in this struggle and that there's a community standing beside us.

So, yeah, being a mortician is no easy gig. The weight of compassion is a burden we bear, but it doesn't have to consume us. Through self-care, reflection, healthy outlets, and support, we can keep doing what we do best - providing the compassionate care that grieving families need. And along the way, we'll carve out some space for our own well-being too.

Moments of Solace

AS A MORTICIAN, I GOTTA tell you, my days are filled with death and grief. It's like a never-ending cycle of heartbreak and tough situations. But let me tell you, finding moments of solace, those little sparks of peace, are what keep me going. They're like my lifeline in all the chaos. Through the years, I've learned a few tricks that help me find solace when the going gets tough.

One of my go-to methods is taking a walk in nature. There's something about being surrounded by the beauty of the natural world that just calms my soul. I remember this one day when the weight of everything was crushing me. The sorrow and grief were suffocating. I needed a break, an escape from it all. So I stepped outside, into the nearby woods. As I strolled through the peaceful forest, with the towering trees and the sweet songs of birds in my ears, a sense of calmness washed over me. Nature became my refuge, a haven where I could escape the chaos and embrace the beauty that still exists, even in the face of death.

Music is another one of my solace secrets. There's something so cathartic about losing myself in soothing melodies and heartfelt lyrics. I remember this one time when I had just finished embalming a child, a tragic loss that hit me hard. The weight of it all was almost unbearable, and grief settled deep in my chest like a heavy stone. To find solace, I retreated to my office, closed my eyes, and played my favorite calming songs. The music filled the room, enveloping me like a warm embrace. The lyrics spoke to my sorrow, and the melodies carried my pain away, if only for a little while. Through the power of music, I could release some of the emotional burden I carried, finding solace and strength in the sound as it washed over me.

I tried to listen to music while I worked on bodies, but, well, let's just say I can't listen to My Chemical Romance's Black Parade album again, such a shame, as I really enjoyed that one.

Sometimes, finding solace is as simple as taking a few deep breaths. In the fast-paced world of my work, it's easy to get lost in the overwhelming emotions and demands. There have been moments when I felt like I couldn't keep my head above water, drowning in sorrow. In those moments, I've learned to anchor myself through the power of deep breaths. I close my eyes, focus on the rise and fall of my chest with every inhale and exhale. With each breath, I let go of a little bit of the burden I'm carrying, finding a moment of solace in the stillness that resides within me.

Finding solace is a must for every mortician. It rejuvenates our hearts and souls, allowing us to offer the highest level of care and compassion to those who have lost loved ones. Through personal stories and chats with my fellow morticians, I've gathered some practical tips for finding solace in the midst of our demanding roles.

First and foremost, we've got to make time for self-care. We're always so busy taking care of others that we forget about ourselves. But carving out time for walks in nature, listening to music, or even just practicing deep breathing exercises, is essential. Even a few minutes each day can make a world of difference in how we handle the challenges we face.

Second, we've got to connect with others who understand what we're going through. Building a strong network of fellow morticians gives us a space to share stories, insights, and coping mechanisms. In these conversations, we find solace in knowing we're not alone in our struggles. Whether it's through support groups or casual get-togethers, the power of sharing our experiences provides a sense of comfort and understanding that can't be beat.

And last, finding solace is an ongoing practice. Life as a mortician is never predictable, and the demands and emotions will keep changing. We've got to keep checking in with ourselves, being aware of what we need emotionally. Being mindful of our own well-being allows us to actively seek solace when we need it most.

So, self-care, connect with others, and find solace. As I say these words, I am sure you have some idea of what you could do for all three.

Once, connecting with others, to me, meant fucking some guy from Tinder who thought it would be extremely hot and sexy to bang a mortician in the back of a hearse. It's not. It's pretty cramped. I'm not Wednesday Addams.

In the end, finding moments of solace amidst the chaos is not just about our own well-being as morticians, it's about the care and comfort we can provide to grieving families. Whether it's through nature walks, listening to music, or focusing on our breath, those little sparks of peace help us recharge our spirits and carry on with strength and compassion. By making self-care a priority, connecting with fellow morticians, and staying mindful, we can find solace in the depths of our work, continuing to serve our communities with grace and empathy.

The Power of Empathy

DEATH IS OUR JOB, YOU know? We're constantly surrounded by grieving families who have lost someone dear to them. And let me tell you, in those moments, empathy becomes our secret weapon in helping these families through the tough process of grief and loss.

When I sit down with a family in mourning, I make sure to really be present with them. I mean, I truly listen to their stories and give them the space to let it all out. It's not enough to just be physically there; I need to actively connect with their pain and show them that I get it. By giving them my full attention, I can let them know that their emotions are real and vital to their healing. It doesn't matter what I'm going through personally. It doesn't matter if a friend is moving and I might not see them again. It doesn't matter if I think I need to take my car in the shop or that the Tinder date got some bodily fluid in the hearse and now I have to clean it before someone sees it. The only thing in the world is that family in mourning.

But empathy doesn't stop there, my friend. It's about offering support without any darn judgment. These families are going through a rollercoaster of emotions, and it can be absolutely overwhelming. Guilt, anger, confusion, emptiness – you name it, they're feeling it. So as morticians, we have a duty to create a safe haven where these emotions can be expressed without any fear of getting criticized or judged. You cannot have an opinion on the way the person died, if they didn't donate organs, what they want their loved one to wear in the casket, nothing.

Now, let me tell you, in all my years in the field, I've seen firsthand how empathy can work its magic. See, when families feel that someone truly sees and hears them, when their pain is acknowledged and understood, that's when the healing starts. It's these moments of genuine connection that make me realize just how powerful empathy can be.

And I'll have you know, research has proven the profound impact of empathetic interactions on both us morticians and the grieving families we work with. For us, it's about gaining a deeper understanding of the human experience and the raw emotions that come with grief. It kind of reminds us to live our lives with more compassion and understanding, you know?

But for the families, the healing potential of empathy is absolutely mind-blowing. Studies have shown that when they feel like someone gets them and supports them, their mental health and overall well-being skyrockets. Empathy gives them the validation and comfort they need to make it through the tough journey of grief and start moving towards healing.

In my line of work, I've personally witnessed the power of empathy in action. By lending an ear, acknowledging their emotions, and offering judgment-free support, I've seen families slowly find the strength to pick up the pieces and heal. And let me tell you, that's a damn beautiful thing to witness.

Oh, and speaking of witnessing, we morticians need to take care of ourselves too. Dealing with death and grief can hit us hard, man, emotionally speaking. So we gotta make self-care a priority. Whether it's hitting the gym, indulging in our passions, or seeking support from fellow morticians or mental health pros, we need to take care of ourselves so we can keep the empathy flowing.

In the end, my friends, never underestimate the power of empathy in our line of work. It allows us to connect with grieving families on a deep level, giving them the comfort and support they so desperately need in their darkest hours. By listening, validating their emotions, and offering that judgment-free support, we create a space of compassion where healing can take place. And heck, that human connection is everything when it comes to dealing with loss.

Navigating Boundaries

IN THE WORLD OF MORTICIANS, boundaries go beyond just physical space. They extend into the realm of emotions and psychology. We have to be aware of the pain and sorrow that surrounds the families we serve, without letting it consume us. It's a delicate balancing act that requires constant self-awareness and self-care. Let me tell you, it's not always easy.

I remember talking to Sarah, a fellow mortician, who opened up about a time when her emotional boundaries were pushed to the limit. She painted a vivid picture of a devastated family who had lost a young child in a tragic accident. The grief wrapped around them like a blanket, and Sarah couldn't help but feel their pain deep within her own heart. It was in that moment that she realized the importance of setting clear boundaries to protect herself.

Sarah knew she needed to create a sacred space within herself where she could hold the pain of others while still honoring her own emotional limits. She started implementing different strategies to achieve this. Taking care of herself became a top priority. Whether it was going for quiet walks in nature, meditating, or indulging in a soothing bubble bath, these moments of solitude allowed her to recharge and replenish her emotional reserves. Sarah learned that by taking care of herself, she could better support others without drowning in their sorrow.

But self-care wasn't the only tool in Sarah's arsenal. She also learned the power of assertive communication in maintaining healthy boundaries. As morticians, it's our responsibility to speak up for ourselves and clearly communicate our needs, all while being respectful. Jasmine, another mortician I spoke with, struggled with this aspect of boundary navigation. She confessed to often accommodating unreasonable demands from grieving families at the expense of her own well-being.

It was during a tough conversation with a client that Jasmine realized she needed assertive communication. The client, consumed by grief, demanded unrealistic timelines and an impossible level of attention. In that moment, Jasmine took a deep breath, mustered her courage, and calmly expressed her constraints and limitations. To her surprise, the client responded with understanding and gratitude. This experience taught Jasmine that setting healthy boundaries not only benefits herself, but also enhances the care and support we can offer to grieving families. By clearly defining what we can and cannot do, we lay the groundwork for a respectful and sustainable relationship with those we serve.

Recognizing the signs of emotional overload is another crucial part of navigating boundaries. As morticians, we dedicate ourselves to being there for people in their darkest hours. It's an honor, but it can also take a toll on our own well-being. That's why it's important to be attuned to the signs of emotional overload and take proactive steps to address them.

I had a conversation with James, a mortician who learned this lesson the hard way. He had been supporting a family who had lost multiple members in a tragic accident. The weight of their grief shook him to the core, and he found himself becoming increasingly distant and detached. James realized that before he could fully be there for others, he needed to seek help for himself.

He reached out to a colleague in grief counseling and started attending therapy sessions. These sessions became a safe space for him to process his own emotions and receive guidance on maintaining healthy boundaries. Through therapy, James discovered the importance of self-reflection and vulnerability in his work. He realized that acknowledging and addressing his own emotional needs wasn't a sign of weakness but rather an act of compassion, both towards himself and the families he served.

Navigating boundaries as a mortician isn't a one-and-done kind of thing. It's a continuous journey that requires us to check in with ourselves, reassess, and recalibrate as needed. It's a delicate dance that blends empathy with detachment, self-care with service. Through the personal stories of morticians like Sarah, Jasmine, and James, we can gain wisdom and inspiration to navigate boundaries with compassion and professionalism.

Their experiences shed light on the complexity of this journey. They provide practical advice on self-care, assertive communication, and recognizing signs of emotional overload. Armed with these tools and the understanding that boundaries are essential for our own well-being and for the care we provide to grieving families, we as morticians are empowered to continue our important work with integrity and compassion.

Coping With Trauma

EVERY SINGLE DAY, I find myself face to face with scenes from the darkest corners of tragedy. Scenes that sear themselves into my memory with the vividness of a razor-sharp knife. It's the raw pain etched into the faces of families as they bid farewell to their loved ones, the gut-wrenching cries of mourners as they surrender to their grief, and the profound sorrow that lingers in the air like a thick fog. Each of these experiences leaves an indelible mark on my soul, exposing me to a secondary trauma that lingers long after the funeral has ended.

The repeated encounters with death and grief have taken their toll on my emotional well-being. I'm hit by a wave of emotions - sadness, anger, and sometimes, even guilt. It's not uncommon for me to question whether I could have done more, or if I made the right decisions in my work as a mortician. These emotions are the natural consequences of the work that we do, and they should never be brushed aside. They need to be acknowledged, confronted, and dealt with.

One thing that I have learned, and is absolutely crucial, is to give myself permission to feel and validate my own emotions. It's so easy to dismiss my own feelings, to see myself as that strong pillar that others depend on. But I've realized that I, too, am vulnerable. Denying my emotions only leads to a buildup of unresolved trauma, a pressure cooker waiting to explode. That's why I've learned to vent, to share my experiences with trusted colleagues or seek the help of a professional therapist. Acknowledging and processing my emotions is essential for my own mental well-being.

I make it a point to engage in activities that bring me joy and comfort, whether it's going for a run, losing myself in a hobby, or simply immersing myself in the soothing embrace of nature. These moments of respite, however short-lived, replenish the emotional resources that I pour into my work. Taking care of myself is not a luxury; it's a necessity, a vital act of self-preservation.

But perhaps one of the most important pieces of the puzzle is seeking support from those who truly understand, who have lived through similar challenges. Connecting with professional organizations or support groups geared towards morticians has shown me that I'm not alone. It's in those connections that I find solace, compassion, and a sense of belonging on this winding journey.

Self-compassion is another crucial ingredient in weathering the storm of trauma. It's so easy to be our own harshest critics, to berate ourselves for feeling what we feel or for the mistakes we think we've made. But I've learned the power of treating myself with kindness and understanding. It's through self-compassion that I heal, that I grow and recognize my own humanity, with all its limitations and its incredible strength.

In the face of trauma, it may be tempting to shut ourselves away, to build walls around our hearts to protect them from further pain. But true resilience lies in our ability to cultivate meaningful connections and relationships. It lies in seeking the support of loved ones who can listen without judgment or simply offer a comforting presence. They remind us of our worth, our capacity for healing, and the immense strength that resides within us.

Coping with trauma as a mortician is an ongoing process, a winding journey that tests our resilience to its core. But by embracing our emotions, seeking support, and practicing self-care, we pave the way for healing and growth. We navigate the treacherous waters of our profession with grace and empathy, while safeguarding our own well-being in the face of darkness.

So, let us remember: coping with trauma as a mortician is no easy feat. The burden we bear is weighty, and the emotional toll is immense. But through acknowledging and processing our own emotions, seeking support, and practicing self-care, we navigate this tumultuous path with resilience and grace. We care for others, and in doing so, we must also care for ourselves, recognizing that we too deserve compassion and healing.

The Toll of the Trade: Recognizing Stress and Compassion Fatigue

The Silent Screams: Unveiling the Hidden Stressors

You know, being a mortician is something else. We're like the guardians of death, kinda poetic if you ask me. Our job isn't just about taking care of the dead, it's about being there for the living left behind too. We see it all, the rawest and most intense grief you can imagine. The screams of pain and sadness, they often get lost in the silence of what we do. But we make it our mission to hold space for the bereaved, to let them know their feelings are valid, and to give them a sense of closure.

But let me tell you, while we're trying to support others, our own well-being can really take a hit. It's not just about lifting bodies, it's about shouldering all the emotions that come with them. Each person we take care of isn't just some life lost, it's a whole story that's ended, a chapter closed forever. And man, those emotions stick with us. They creep into our souls and leave us haunted by silent screams.

It's not just about the physical weight of the deceased, you know. It's about their stories, their relationships, the huge responsibility we carry to honor their memory. We are the keepers of their final moments, tasked with bringing dignity and respect to their goodbye. But in doing that, we become so attached to their stories. We carry around all the unfinished business, the unspoken words, the promises unfulfilled that death left behind.

Now, let me tell you about funeral processions. They may be dignified and somber, but they can be a real emotional rollercoaster for us morticians. Seeing those grieving families, saying their final goodbyes, it hits us hard. We feel the weight of their sorrow in our own hearts, like their tears reverberating through our souls. We're silently there, supporting them, even as our own hearts ache in solidarity.

And it's not just the deceased and their families that affect us. It's the constant demands of our job, the pressure to be flawless and composed in the face of death. It takes a toll on our mental and emotional well-being, let me tell you. Balancing professionalism with our own vulnerabilities, it's a tough act to maintain. Our own silent screams of exhaustion and inner turmoil go unnoticed, buried under the weight of expectations and the mask we wear.

But in the peace of the mortuary, it's like the walls hold our unspoken fears. We find solace in the quiet moments, where the scent of embalming fluid mixes with our own thoughts. That's when the silent screams of our profession really hit us. It's a reminder of how elusive our work is, and how death is something we all have to face eventually.

By shining a light on the hidden stressors of our job, we can finally acknowledge the impact it has on us. It's not just a nine-to-five gig, it's a calling that asks for unwavering compassion and resilience. We gotta remember to take care of ourselves, to tend to our own wounds caused by all this invisible stress. And by speaking up about the silent screams that fill the mortuary, we make room for healing and growth. Not just for ourselves, but for every mortician out there carrying the weight of other people's sorrow.

Beyond the Job: Navigating Personal Boundaries

UNDERSTANDING THE IMPORTANCE of setting boundaries in my personal and professional life didn't exactly come naturally to me, let me tell you. Like a lot of folks in this line of work, I was drawn to the mortuary biz because I wanted to be there for people in their darkest moments. I wanted to offer them some comfort and support when they needed it most. And boy, did it give me a sense of purpose. But it didn't take long for me to realize that constantly being surrounded by grief could really mess with my own emotions.

There's this one incident that's forever etched in my memory. It was a hot summer evening and I got a call about a terrible car accident that took the lives of a young couple. When I got to the scene, the atmosphere was heavy with sorrow as the families gathered, their anguish practically hanging in the air. Even though I was surrounded by heartbreak, I focused on my duty to help these folks through their unimaginable loss.

Days turned into nights, and I worked my butt off to get everything ready for the memorial service. The weight of grief just settled onto my shoulders, invading my thoughts and feelings. And as the days blended together, I realized that I had lost sight of myself. I had become so consumed by death and sadness that I barely recognized who I was anymore. It was like I had forgotten how to take care of myself.

That's when it hit me – if I wanted to be the best damn caretaker for others, I had to create some space for myself to heal and recover, to be my own caretaker. And so, I set off on this journey of self-discovery. I carved out time just for me, making self-care a non-negotiable part of my day. Mornings became sacred moments for meditation and reflection, and walks in nature became my way of rejuvenating my weary soul. These moments of solitude gave me the strength I needed to face the challenges of my job.

But finding solace in the company of others who understood my struggles was just as vital. Connecting with fellow morticians who knew exactly what we were dealing with created this support network that extended beyond the workplace. We shared our experiences, leaned on each other, and reminded ourselves that our own well-being mattered just as much as the families we served.

It wasn't just about finding support, though. I also had to change my mindset about being a mortician. Instead of seeing death as a constant reminder of mortality, I started to see the beauty and honor in the work I did. Every life

I had the privilege to care for held a special story, and by celebrating their lives, I found a sense of peace and purpose.

This personal growth journey also taught me some practical tips for preserving my own sanity while serving others. I learned the power of setting clear boundaries with my clients and colleagues, making sure I had time to recharge and renew. Saying "no" didn't mean I wasn't dedicated or compassionate. It just meant I wanted to be present and effective in my work.

Creating rituals and practices that kept me grounded in the present moment also became essential. From journaling my thoughts and emotions at the end of the day to practicing mindfulness exercises regularly, these intentional acts became my lifeline. They reminded me that my own well-being wasn't a luxury – it was a necessity.

As morticians, we'll forever be walking a tightrope between caring for others and caring for ourselves. It's all about finding that balance where we can flourish in this profession we've chosen. By setting boundaries and finding moments of rest, we not only become better at providing solace but also honor our own humanity. We navigate the tricky realm of personal boundaries, finding the strength to face the realities of our work while also taking care of ourselves.

Just like the barber who needs someone else to cut their hair, one day, we too will need a mortician of our own.

When Empathy Becomes Exhaustion: The

Perils of Compassion Fatigue

YOU KNOW, THEY SAY that empathy is pretty much the backbone of being a mortician. We're the ones who are there to support people when they're grieving, lending an ear to their stories, and giving them some comfort in those dark times. But you know what happens when empathy takes over way too much? It turns into something called compassion fatigue. And trust me, it's a real pain in the you-know-where.

In this little adventure, I want you to come along with me as we untangle the mess of compassion fatigue and see how it messes with us morticians. We'll hear some real-life stories and get some expert insights too. But the best part is that we're going to figure out how to take care of ourselves and get back to being the best support we can for others. It's about time we prioritize our own well-being while we continue to be there for everyone else.

Now, compassion fatigue isn't some newfangled idea, but it's something that often goes overlooked in our field. We're so used to putting everyone else's needs before our own that we don't even notice when we're about to crash and burn. But let me tell you, ignoring compassion fatigue doesn't end well, for both us and the families we serve.

One of the major signs of compassion fatigue is feeling emotionally exhausted, drained to the core. It's like a never-ending cycle of being physically and mentally wiped out from all the intense emotions we deal with every day. The stories of tragedy and heartbreak can really do a number on even the toughest of souls. No wonder so many of us feel overwhelmed and empty.

But listen, compassion fatigue ain't just about being tired. It shows itself in lots of other ways too. Trouble sleeping, loss of appetite, irritability, and just not being happy with our job anymore are just some of the signs that start popping up. We start distancing ourselves emotionally from our families and colleagues, feeling like we're disconnected from everything around us. Trust me, those signs are big ol' red flags telling us to slow down and start taking care of ourselves.

Now, let's get real and hear the stories of some of our fellow morticians. Take Sarah, for example. She's got years of experience as a funeral director, but lately, she's been feeling burnt out. She used to love her job, but now it's like she's slowly losing herself. She listens to people's stories of grief, tries to hold back the tears, and puts on a brave face. But when she's alone, it's like all that sadness and loss has taken over her. It's a heavy burden to carry, you know?

And I bet Sarah's story hits close to home for a bunch of us. We get so deep into other people's pain that it becomes our own. On top of that, we forget to take care of ourselves and push ourselves to the breaking point just to help others. But here's the thing: we can't pour from an empty cup. If we don't look after ourselves, we won't be able to give the support and compassion that our families need so badly.

Compassion fatigue, also known as secondary traumatic stress or empathic burnout, is a term used to describe the emotional and physical exhaustion that can result from consistently caring for and supporting others who are experiencing trauma or suffering. This condition is often associated with healthcare professionals, first responders, social workers, caregivers, and anyone in roles that require continuous empathy and support for individuals in distress. Compassion fatigue can have a profound impact on one's well-being, making it crucial to recognize its signs and take steps to combat it.

Signs of Compassion Fatigue:

- Emotional exhaustion: You may feel drained and overwhelmed by the emotional demands of your job or caregiving role.

- Reduced empathy: Over time, you might become less sensitive to the suffering of others, which can lead to feelings of guilt.

- Increased cynicism: You may become more critical or pessimistic, leading to a negative outlook on your work and life in general.

- Physical symptoms: Compassion fatigue can manifest in physical symptoms like headaches, sleep disturbances, and gastrointestinal issues.

- Decreased job satisfaction: You might experience a decline in job performance and job satisfaction.

• Isolation and withdrawal: You may distance yourself from friends and loved ones, leading to social isolation.

Combatting Compassion Fatigue:

• Self-care: Prioritize self-care activities that promote physical, emotional, and mental well-being. This includes maintaining a balanced diet, regular exercise, sufficient sleep, and relaxation techniques like meditation or yoga.

• Boundaries: Set clear and healthy boundaries to avoid overextending yourself. Learn to say "no" when necessary and communicate your limitations to others.

• Seek support: Share your feelings and experiences with trusted friends, family, or colleagues. Support groups and professional therapists can provide a safe space to discuss your emotions.

• Mindfulness and stress management: Develop mindfulness techniques to manage stress and maintain emotional balance. This can involve deep breathing exercises, progressive muscle relaxation, or other stress reduction strategies.

• Rotate responsibilities: If possible, distribute responsibilities among a team or caregivers to prevent burnout. Sharing the emotional burden can help each individual better cope.

● Take breaks: Regularly schedule short breaks to recharge during the day, and plan longer periods of respite, such as vacations, to disconnect and rejuvenate.

● Professional development: Invest in continuous education and training to enhance your coping strategies and resilience in the face of challenging situations.

● Reflect and debrief: Regularly engage in reflective practices to process your experiences. Debrief with colleagues or supervisors to share insights and seek guidance.

● Practice self-compassion: Be as kind and understanding to yourself as you are to those you care for. Acknowledge your own needs and prioritize self-compassion.

● Monitor for signs: Regularly assess your emotional state and well-being. Early recognition of compassion fatigue symptoms allows for timely intervention.

Compassion fatigue is a significant concern for those in caregiving professions, but with proactive self-care and support, individuals can effectively combat its effects. It's essential to recognize that taking care of oneself is not a sign of weakness but a vital aspect of sustaining the ability to provide empathy and support to others in need.

That's why, my friends, we need to make self-care and renewal our top priority. It might feel like we're being selfish, but it's a necessary step if we want to keep ourselves going strong. Self-care can be different for everyone, so find what nourishes your body, mind, and spirit. Whether it's working out, getting creative, or seeking help from a therapist, make time to recharge and replenish yourself.

And let me tell you, self-care isn't a luxury. It's a responsibility. When we take care of ourselves, we're making sure that we can still be there for our families with empathy and understanding. We owe it to ourselves and to our profession to put our well-being first, even in the face of immense grief and loss.

So come on, join me on this journey of self-discovery and healing. Let's reclaim our own well-being while still being that pillar of support for others. We'll remember the importance of compassion in our line of work, but this time, we won't forget to take care of our own hearts. It's time to leave that heavy burden of compassion fatigue behind and embrace a renewed sense of purpose and vitality.

The Weight of Loss: Coping With Grief as a Mortician

BEING A MORTICIAN, let me tell you, it's not a job you stumble into by accident. You can't just wake up one day and think, "Hey, being around dead bodies sounds like a blast!" No, my friend, it takes a certain kind of person to enter this line of work. Someone who understands death, who can empathize with the bereft, and who can provide solace when tragedy strikes. And let me tell you, every single day, we face mortality like a boxer in the ring, taking punch after punch, witnessing firsthand the devastating impact of loss. It's heavy stuff, my friend.

But here's the thing: we're not just stone-cold professionals. We're human, too. We feel the weight of loss deep in our bones. We experience grief, sometimes quietly, sometimes privately, as we process the lives that have passed through our hands. It's a burden, my friend, because even though we're there to comfort others, we have to face our own emotions head-on and find a way to navigate the choppy waters of grief.

Let me tell you a bit about my own journey as a mortician. Oh boy, it's been a rollercoaster ride of loss and personal growth. I've learned that it's important to acknowledge and validate my own damn emotions, just like I do for the families I serve. Ignoring my grief would be like sticking my hand in a pot of boiling water – it would just keep burning and burning until I couldn't take it anymore. And that would be a disservice to everyone I'm trying to help.

One of the biggest lessons I've learned is the power of vulnerability. Back in the day, I thought I had to be a stone-cold statue, unaffected by grief. I thought showing my own sadness would be unprofessional, like I couldn't do my job properly if I shed a tear. But lemme tell ya, vulnerability ain't weakness. It's a strength, my friend. By sharing my own experiences of loss and grief, I create an open space for families to express themselves. They see that it's okay to feel all sorts of things when someone they love passes away.

Now, I gotta tell you about finding healthy outlets for our own grief. 'Cause let me tell ya, I've found mine, and it's writing. I take the time, every day, to sit down with my notepad and let it all out. I spill my emotions onto the page so I don't carry them around like a loaded backpack. You know, it's like a pressure release valve, and it keeps me sane in this crazy world.

But you know what else helps? Talking to my fellow morticians. And not just us dark souls, but mental health professionals too. Having a support network is like a lifeline in this gig. It helps us see that we're not alone in our struggles, that there are others out there who carry the same weight on their shoulders. It gives us validation and a real sense of connection as we face the unique challenges of our profession.

And here's the thing, buddy: self-care ain't some fancy luxury. It's an absolute must for us morticians. We've gotta prioritize our own well-being so we can keep being there for others. So, I make time for things that bring me joy and help me reflect. Maybe it's hitting the gym, or meditating, or just taking a long walk in nature. Whatever gets my spirits up and replenishes my emotional fuel tank, that's what I do.

At the end of the day, my friend, we gotta remember not to let the weight of loss crush us. We've gotta make space for our own grief while still being there for those who need us most. It's a delicate balance, but by being vulnerable, seeking support, and taking care of ourselves, we can navigate this dance between sorrow and compassion. And in doing so, we honor our own healing and the legacy of those we've lost. It ain't an easy road, my friend, but it's one worth walking.

Building Resilience: Strengthening the Mind and Spirit

YOU KNOW, ONE OF THE first things we gotta do if we wanna keep our sanity in this mortician gig is to take care of ourselves. It's easy to get caught up in looking after everyone else and forget about our own needs. But let me tell you, neglecting ourselves can really take a toll and before we know it, we're burnt out and feeling like we've run out of compassion. So, it's time to stop, take a breath, and make self-care a priority.

Now, I know our schedules are jam-packed and it feels impossible to find a minute for ourselves. But trust me, we gotta make that time. Even just a few minutes each day can make a world of difference. We need to find ways to focus on our own emotional well-being. And you know what? Mindfulness exercises can totally help with that.

Mindfulness is like a secret weapon, my friend. It helps us stay present and aware of our emotions without drowning in them. It's all about observing our thoughts and feelings without any judgment. And let me tell you, it's a game-changer when it comes to managing stress and tough emotions. Once we've got that inner awareness going, we can start recognizing when we're running on empty and take steps to recharge our batteries.

But hey, mindfulness ain't the only trick up our sleeves. Self-reflection exercises can be pretty darn valuable too. I'm talking about taking a moment to think about our experiences and emotions. It helps us process the challenges we face and understand ourselves on a deeper level. When we're aware of any negative thinking or unhealthy coping mechanisms, we can start kicking them to the curb. It's all about shifting our mindset to one of gratitude and resilience, my friend.

Oh, and don't get me started on positive affirmations! These babies are like fuel for our minds and spirits. When we repeat positive statements to ourselves, like "I am resilient" or "I can handle anything life throws at me," our brains start to believe it. It's like we're rewiring ourselves to focus on our own strengths instead of getting sucked into the difficulties of our job.

And speaking of focusing on ourselves, we need to nurture our relationships with our fellow morticians. They get it, you know? There's something comforting about connecting with people who truly understand what we're going through.

Sharing our struggles and successes with them not only makes us feel less alone, but it also gives us some valuable insights and advice. It's like having our very own support system on standby.

Of course, self-care activities are a must. We need to recharge and reconnect with ourselves regularly. It can be as simple as taking a stroll in nature, diving into a hobby, or getting our bodies moving. These activities are like a breath of fresh air, a break from the intense demands of our work. When we make self-care a priority, we're replenishing our energy and building that resilience we so desperately need.

As morticians, we navigate the delicate and often emotionally charged world of death and bereavement daily. Our role involves providing essential services, support, and comfort to grieving families, and it's a profession that requires a unique combination of empathy, professionalism, and resilience. Mindfulness, the practice of being fully present and aware in the moment, can be a valuable tool to help us cope with the emotional demands of our work while maintaining our own well-being.

Here's how mindfulness can benefit morticians:

- Emotional Resilience: Mindfulness can help you manage the intense emotions that often accompany your work. It allows you to acknowledge your feelings without judgment and helps prevent emotional burnout.

• Improved Focus: Mindfulness helps you stay fully engaged in the tasks at hand, ensuring that you provide the best care and support to grieving families. Being present in the moment can enhance your attention to detail and professionalism.

• Reduced Stress: The practice of mindfulness has been shown to reduce stress and anxiety. Morticians can benefit from these techniques to maintain their own mental health, even in the face of distressing situations.

• Empathy: Mindfulness fosters a sense of empathy and compassion. By being more in tune with your own emotions, you become better at understanding and supporting the emotions of others.

• Effective Communication: Mindfulness can improve communication skills, helping you to listen more attentively and respond more effectively to the needs and concerns of grieving families.

Here are some ways morticians can incorporate mindfulness into our lives:

• Mindful Breathing: Take a moment to focus on your breath. Pay attention to the sensation of each inhalation and exhalation. This simple practice can help you center yourself and relieve stress.

● Mindful Breaks: Throughout your workday, take short breaks to step outside, stretch, or simply pause and be present. These moments of mindfulness can help you reset and recharge.

● Meditation: Consider incorporating regular meditation sessions into your daily routine, even if it's just for a few minutes. Meditation can enhance your mindfulness skills and provide a sense of inner calm.

● Mindful Listening: When speaking with grieving families, practice active listening. Be fully present during these conversations, giving them your undivided attention.

● Mindful Grief Processing: Allow yourself time to grieve and process the emotions that may arise from your work. Share your experiences with colleagues or seek support when needed.

● Professional Boundaries: Mindfulness can help you establish and maintain professional boundaries while still offering empathy and support. It can prevent emotional entanglement with the families you serve.

• Self-Care: Prioritize self-care activities such as exercise, healthy eating, and sufficient sleep. A healthy body supports a healthy mind.

• Mindful Rituals: Incorporate mindfulness into your work rituals. Whether it's preparing a body for a service or conducting a ceremony, do so with a mindful presence and intention.

Mindfulness can be a powerful tool for morticians, enabling them to provide compassionate and professional care while safeguarding their own emotional well-being. By incorporating these practices into your daily routine, you can find a sense of balance in the face of death and continue to support those in need with grace and empathy.

But here's the thing we often forget: we're not superheroes. We gotta acknowledge and accept our limitations. It's true, we wanna be there for grieving families, but we can't fix everything. We're only human, with our own vulnerabilities and boundaries. It's crucial to set those boundaries, to avoid getting overwhelmed, and to maintain our own well-being.

In the end, building resilience is essential for us morticians to keep going strong in this tough profession. So, let's get on board with mindfulness, self-reflection, positive affirmations, support networks, self-care, and embracing our limitations. These are the things that'll strengthen our minds and spirits. They'll help us keep that compassion and grace, even when we face death and sorrow every day. When we take care of ourselves, we can provide the care and support grieving families need while still protecting our own emotional well-being.

Self-Awareness: The First Step to Self-Care

The Mirror of Self-Reflection

Self-reflection, man, it's been around forever. Like, since way back in the day. People like Socrates and Plato from ancient Greece and those dudes who were into Buddhism and Taoism, they all knew what was up. They were all about understanding themselves and growing as humans through self-reflection. And you know what? That's still important today, even in our crazy, fast-paced world.

These days, though, it's easy to forget about self-reflection. We're so caught up in our phones and everything that's going on around us. It's like we never have a chance to just sit and think. As morticians, though, it's like a requirement. We gotta take the time to look inside ourselves and figure out what's going on.

When we do that, it's like looking in a mirror, but, you know, a mirror for our thoughts and feelings. No judgment, no attachments. Just sitting with ourselves and being curious about who we are. It's a chance to get some insight into why we're so stressed and burnt out, and maybe even find ways to take care of ourselves better.

There are lots of ways to do self-reflection. Some people write in a journal, just dumping all their thoughts onto the page. Others meditate or practice mindfulness to focus on what's going on inside. And hey, some people even get creative with it, like painting or dancing. As long as we make the time and find a space for it, any method works.

The important thing is to have that sacred time for self-reflection. No distractions, no interruptions. Just us and our own minds. Even if it's just a few minutes a day, that sends a message that we matter. And in that space, we can really dive deep and get to know ourselves better.

Now, I'm not gonna lie, self-reflection can get tough. We might uncover some truths we'd rather not face. But instead of running away, we need to show ourselves some understanding and compassion. We're human, after all, and we all have our flaws. It's through that compassion that we can grow and heal.

As we keep going with our self-reflection, we might start to see patterns and themes in our thoughts and emotions. It's like a clue to who we are deep down. Knowing those patterns empowers us to make better choices and break free from negative cycles. It's all about finding healthier ways of being.

And self-reflection isn't just about awareness. It also helps us figure out how to take care of ourselves. It's about knowing what we really need. That way, our self-care routines are actually serving us, not just going through the motions. We gotta nourish our minds, bodies, and souls for real.

But the best part of self-reflection is that it lets us connect with ourselves on a deeper level. We can accept who we are and love ourselves, flaws and all. That kind of relationship with ourselves is like a source of strength. It helps us handle whatever comes our way, and it keeps us going in this crazy mortician life.

A mirror of self-reflection exercise for morticians can be a profound and contemplative practice that draws inspiration from both Buddhist and Taoist philosophies. This exercise goes beyond the conventional aspects of their profession, encouraging a deeper exploration of the nature of life, death, and the impermanence of existence.

Mirror of Self-Reflection Exercise:

1. Setting the Stage: Begin by creating a quiet and serene space, free from distractions. This could be a dedicated room or a corner within the mortuary. Lighting candles or incense can help set a meditative atmosphere.

2. Facing the Mirror: Stand in front of a mirror, symbolizing self-reflection. The mirror represents the impermanence of life and the reflection of one's own mortality. As morticians often deal with death on a daily basis, this exercise aims to provoke deeper thoughts about the transience of existence.

3. Breath Awareness: Start with mindful breathing. Focus on each breath, bringing attention to the present moment. This practice aligns with mindfulness principles found in both Buddhist and Taoist traditions, emphasizing the importance of being fully present.

4. Contemplating Impermanence: Look at your reflection and contemplate the impermanence of both life and the physical body. In Buddhism, the concept of impermanence (Anicca) is fundamental, highlighting the inevitability of change. Taoism also acknowledges the natural cycle of life and death, encouraging individuals to flow with the rhythm of existence.

5. Reflection on Compassion: Consider the compassion required in the mortician's role. Reflect on the interconnectedness of all life and the shared human experience of mortality. This aligns with the Buddhist principle of compassion (Karuna) and the Taoist idea of living in harmony with nature and humanity.

6. Letting Go of Attachment: In both Buddhist and Taoist philosophies, there is an emphasis on letting go of attachments. As a mortician, the exercise involves reflecting on detachment from the physical form and acknowledging the transient nature of the body.

7. Gratitude and Service: Express gratitude for the opportunity to serve others during times of grief. Connect this sense of service with the Buddhist concept of Right Livelihood and the Taoist idea of living a life of virtue and purpose.

8. Integrating Insights: Take the insights gained from this reflective exercise into your daily life and professional practice. Embrace the teachings of impermanence, compassion, and detachment as

you navigate the challenges of working with the deceased and supporting grieving families.

By integrating elements of Buddhist and Taoist philosophies into this mirror of self-reflection exercise, morticians can cultivate a holistic perspective on life and death, finding meaning and purpose in their unique role within the cycle of existence.

So, my friends, let's make time for self-reflection. It's how we cope with all the stress and burnout that comes with our job. It's how we get to know ourselves and take better care of ourselves. It's how we live a healthier, more fulfilling life. So let's go ahead and look in that mirror of self-reflection. Embrace the power it brings.

Unmasking the Mask

YOU KNOW, IN OUR LINE of work, we morticians are taught to put on a brave face, to stay composed and professional in the face of death. We become masters at hiding our emotions, pushing aside our own grief, and focusing solely on the needs of the grieving. That mask becomes our lifeline, protecting us from the overwhelming emotions that surround us every day. It's like a suit of armor, guarding our hearts and minds from the constant reminder of our own mortality.

But my friend, deep down, hidden beneath that mask, there's a vulnerability lurking. Our work exposes us to the fragile nature of life, the pain of loss, and the heavy burden of grief.

You see, even us morticians have a whole range of emotions swirling inside. We crave connection and understanding, even though society expects us to maintain an unflinching facade of stoicism.

And those masks, they don't just stop us from showing our true selves. They also make it hard for us to connect with others on a deeper level. We become masters at building walls, shutting ourselves off from the world, scared to let anyone in. We worry that if we take off our masks, people will see us as weak, and our vulnerabilities will overshadow our professionalism. But let me tell you something, my friend, it's through vulnerability that real connections and healing can happen.

To unmask ourselves, we need to embark on a journey of self-reflection. We have to dig deep and unravel the layers of our identity. Why do we wear these masks? Is it fear? Is it the need for control? Or maybe we've just been conditioned to think that emotions have no place in our line of work. Whatever the reason, we have to face it head-on, one layer at a time.

I won't lie to you; this process won't be easy. It's going to push us out of our comfort zones, force us to confront our fears and insecurities. As we peel back those layers, we may unearth a mix of emotions buried deep within. Grief, guilt, and even trauma might be waiting for us. But my friend, it's crucial that we give ourselves permission to feel all of it, to acknowledge its existence without judgment.

Through this unmasking process, we'll discover the power of embracing our true selves. When we let our authentic selves be seen and understood, we create space for healing and growth. No longer do we have to carry the burden of pretense. Instead, we can be real and connect with others on a whole new level. By removing our masks, we break down the walls that separate us and foster a community of support within our industry.

And let me tell you, unveiling our true selves also has a tremendous impact on our well-being. When we wear masks, we bear the weight of emotional labor alone. We internalize the grief and trauma, carrying it with us long after we leave the mortuary. But when we embrace our authentic selves, we invite others to share in that emotional journey, lightening the load and creating a support network. Through vulnerability and openness, we find solace in the understanding and empathy of others.

Now, my friend, unmasking ourselves is not a one-time event. It's an ongoing process that requires constant self-reflection and a commitment to authenticity. There will be days when the mask feels necessary, when the weight of our work is just too heavy. And that's okay. We get to decide when to don the mask and when to let ourselves be seen. But by acknowledging the mask's existence and approaching it with compassion, we start chipping away at its power over us.

We morticians have become experts at wearing the mask, but behind those masks are real people yearning to be seen and understood. Through introspection and vulnerability, we can uncover the layers of our true identity. We learn that it's crucial to embrace our authentic selves, not just for our own well-being, but for the collective healing and support within our industry. So let's do it, my friend. It's time to unmask ourselves and let our true selves shine, lighting the way to a healthier and more fulfilling life.

Embracing Vulnerability: The Strength in Sensitivity

YOU KNOW, IN A WORLD that's all about being tough and stoic, it can be pretty tough to let ourselves be vulnerable. We're scared of being seen as weak or incompetent, so we put on this brave face and hide our true emotions. But by doing that, we miss out on genuine connections and the chance to fully experience what it means to be human.

Now, vulnerability doesn't mean we're weak or fragile. It means we're willing to acknowledge and share our emotions, fears, and weaknesses with others. It means opening up about our struggles and pain, knowing that it's through this act that we can find support and strength. Have you ever noticed that when you allow yourself to be vulnerable, others feel more comfortable doing the same? It's like this chain reaction of compassion and understanding.

But how the heck do we embrace vulnerability in a job that demands strength and composure? How do we walk that fine line between being sensitive to others' needs while also taking care of ourselves? Well, my friend, it's all about recognizing that vulnerability and strength aren't enemies - they're two sides of the same coin.

I remember when I first started out in this line of work, feeling completely overwhelmed by the weight of it all. The pain and loss I witnessed on a daily basis started to chip away at my composure. It was during that time that I discovered just how powerful it can be to embrace vulnerability.

I started by allowing myself to actually feel and acknowledge my own emotions. Instead of hiding them away, I let myself cry, grieve, and process the losses I was witnessing. You know what happened? Not only did I give myself permission to be human, but I also gained a deeper understanding of the pain my clients were going through.

Okay, so let's get practical for a second. This next part is all about exercises and anecdotes that can help you embrace vulnerability and find strength in your sensitivity. Trust me, it's worth it. We'll explore how vulnerability plays a role in developing resilience and compassion, and we'll learn how to strike that delicate balance between strength and sensitivity.

One game-changer for me was creating a safe space for vulnerability. It sounds simple, I know, but setting aside a few minutes each day to check in with yourself and really feel your emotions can make a world of difference. Find a quiet place, close your eyes, and let yourself become aware of what you're feeling. No judgment, no criticism - just observe and let it be. This practice of self-reflection and acceptance is a powerful tool for connecting with your own vulnerability and fostering compassion for yourself.

But don't stop there - reach out to others for support. Talk to colleagues, mentors, or seek out support groups specifically for folks in our line of work. Surround yourself with people who get it, who understand the unique challenges we face, and who can lend an ear or some words of encouragement when needed. Remember, vulnerability thrives in connection, and asking for support just strengthens our own resilience.

Now listen up: embracing vulnerability is a journey, not an overnight fix. There will be times when you still struggle to fully open yourself up or when your emotions overwhelm you. But with practice and a little self-compassion, you'll start to navigate that delicate balance between strength and sensitivity.

To wrap things up, let's be crystal clear: embracing vulnerability is not a sign of weakness. It's a source of incredible strength and growth. By allowing ourselves to be vulnerable, we create genuine connections with others and gain a deeper understanding of our own humanity. So, my friend, let's take that courageous step towards embracing vulnerability and empower ourselves to provide compassionate care while keeping our own well-being intact.

The Dance of Boundaries: How to Say No With Grace

YOU KNOW, SETTING BOUNDARIES isn't about being selfish or not caring about others. It's actually a way to protect ourselves. It's acknowledging our own limitations and respecting our own needs. So, by setting boundaries, we're basically giving ourselves permission to take care of ourselves without sacrificing the quality of our work or relationships.

But man, getting started on this journey of establishing healthy boundaries means we gotta be okay with saying no. Society loves to praise those who always say yes, like they're these selfless heroes. But hey, we've got our own lives to live, our own struggles to face, and our own stuff to focus on. Saying no is like taking back our power and saying, "Hey, I matter too."

So how can we say no in a smooth and graceful way? Well, effective communication is key. We've gotta be clear and straightforward when expressing our boundaries. No beating around the bush or giving vague answers. We need to speak up assertively and honestly. By being upfront about our limits, we're giving others a chance to understand and respect our boundaries.

One trick to saying no gracefully is offering alternatives or compromises. Let's say a coworker asks us to take on another task that we just can't handle right now. We can suggest helping them out later or even recommend someone else who might be available. By providing other solutions, we're showing that we care about the relationship and finding ways to support each other without burning ourselves out.

And don't forget, we've gotta be our own advocates too. We gotta stand up for ourselves and our needs, even when the pressure is on or guilt trips are being laid on thick. It takes a strong sense of self-worth and trusting our own judgment. By standing up for ourselves, we're setting the tone for how others should treat us and making sure our needs are met.

But here's the thing, setting boundaries is an ongoing thing. As morticians, we're constantly dealing with emotional and psychological stress. Our boundaries might need tweaking or adjusting as circumstances change or as we grow personally. It's important to be flexible while still taking care of ourselves. Boundaries aren't something to be rigid about; they require self-awareness and self-care in our line of work.

And let's not get it twisted, setting boundaries doesn't mean shutting ourselves off or disconnecting from our work. It's actually the opposite. It allows us to be fully present and engaged when we do say yes. By taking care of ourselves and honoring our own needs, we can show up as the best versions of ourselves for our clients and colleagues. Our empathy and compassion won't be diminished; it'll actually be heightened because we know we're taking care of ourselves.

So bottom line, this whole dance of boundaries is a vital part of self-care for us morticians. It's that delicate balance between looking out for ourselves and fulfilling our professional duties. By learning to say no with grace and communicating our boundaries effectively, we can make self-care a priority without sacrificing the quality of our work or relationships. And let's not forget, setting boundaries isn't selfish at all; it's a way of preserving ourselves. It's a way of showing our commitment to our well-being and the longevity of our profession. So embrace the dance of boundaries and take back your power to prioritize your own self-care.

The Whispers of Intuition: Trusting Our Inner Guidance

LET'S START BY TALKING about embracing solitude. In the midst of our crazy busy lives, finding some moments of peace and quiet is key to reconnecting with our intuition. It's in those quiet spaces that we can finally tune out all the external noise and truly hear what our inner voice is trying to tell us. Whether it's taking a leisurely walk in nature or finding that cozy corner at home, embracing solitude gives our intuition the space it needs to thrive.

I remember a time when my work was driving me nuts. I was on the verge of burnout, so I decided to escape to a secluded cabin deep in the woods. Surrounded by nature's calming presence, I finally found some peace and quiet. Away from the constant phone calls and the buzz of everyday life, I could finally tune in to my intuition. And you know what? In those moments, I felt this newfound clarity and a heightened awareness of what I truly needed and desired.

Now, let's talk about the importance of stillness. Quieting the mind is like unlocking the superpowers of our intuition. Our minds are so often flooded with thoughts and external influences that it can be hard to hear that inner guidance. But cultivating a practice of stillness can create an environment where our intuition can really shine.

Meditation is a game-changer here. Finding a comfy spot, closing your eyes, and focusing on your breath can help you enter a state of peaceful observation. This is where the magic happens. As your mind settles, you start to tap into your intuitive wisdom.

I know, silencing the mind can be pretty intimidating, especially for those of us used to the constant hustle of our day-to-day lives. But trust me, with practice, our minds become more attuned to silence, and the whispers of our intuition become crystal clear. The more we embrace stillness, the more we trust the guidance of our inner voice.

For me, journaling has been an absolute lifeline. Every day, I take a few minutes to sit with my thoughts and let them flow onto the pages of my journal. As I write, I notice those subtle nudges from my intuition guiding my hand and revealing hidden truths. Through this practice, I've developed a deeper understanding of who I am and have been able to make decisions that are aligned with my authentic self.

Finally, we've gotta talk about trusting the whispers of our intuition. It's an ongoing process that requires us to build a deep sense of self-trust and belief in our inner wisdom. It's not always easy, especially in a society that values logic and rationality over those gentle nudges from our inner voice. But when we learn to trust those whispers, a whole new world of possibilities opens up, and we find true fulfillment.

As morticians, we face some pretty complex decisions and choices that impact not only our own well-being but also the lives of the people we serve. That's where our intuition comes in handy. By trusting our inner guidance, we can make decisions that are compassionate and nurturing. It's all about honoring our values, staying true to our authentic selves, and ultimately leading a purposeful life.

To sum it all up, in the fast-paced and demanding world of mortuary work, reconnecting with our intuition is an absolute must. By embracing solitude, cultivating a quiet mind, journaling, and trusting the whispers of our inner guidance, we can tap into the transformative power of our intuition. And let me tell you, it's not just about nurturing our own well-being. It's about becoming better caregivers and advocates for the families we serve. So, let's embark on this journey of self-discovery and allow our intuition to be the guiding light that leads us to a truly fulfilling and purposeful life.

Boundaries and Balance: Navigating the Work-Life Equation

Setting Boundaries: Protecting Your Emotional Well-being

Hey there! In this subchapter, I'm gonna take you on a journey - my personal journey, to be exact - where I learned a thing or two about setting boundaries and protecting my emotional well-being in the mortuary profession. Trust me, it wasn't an easy road, but I'm gonna share some practical tips on how you can establish healthy limits without sacrificing that good ol' compassion and empathy. So, sit back, relax, and join me as we dive into the importance of self-care and the power of saying 'no' when you need to.

Now, as morticians, our world revolves around death and grief. It's our job to provide comfort and support to mourning families during their darkest moments. But let me tell you, being surrounded by all those intense emotions can really take a toll on our own well-being if we're not careful.

Back when I was just starting out in this line of work, I had this naive idea that helping others meant completely neglecting my own emotional needs. I thought I had an endless capacity to absorb the pain of others, but boy was I wrong. That mindset led to nothing but burnout and compassion fatigue. It took one heartbreaking case - a child's death - for me to realize the weight of my emotional exhaustion. I was sinking into a deep emotional abyss, and that's when I knew something had to change.

I started by becoming more self-aware and accepting my own emotional limitations. I discovered that taking care of myself wasn't selfish at all. In fact, it actually made me a better support system for those grieving families. It was a mindset shift that allowed me to shed the guilt that came with setting boundaries.

But let me tell you, setting those boundaries wasn't a walk in the park. Funeral homes are always buzzing, and death never follows a set schedule. Learning to say 'no' felt like such a betrayal to those who needed me the most. But here's the thing - constantly saying 'yes' was a recipe for disaster.

So, what did I do? Well, I started by creating a schedule that allowed me to take regular breaks and some much-needed time off. Having set hours for myself didn't mean that I cared any less for the families I served. It simply meant that I cared for myself enough to show up for them when they needed me most. I made sure to designate specific times during the day for self-care activities like exercise, meditation, and journaling. Those moments allowed me to recharge my emotional batteries, ya know?

In addition to setting aside time for myself, I also discovered the importance of setting emotional boundaries. As morticians, we have this uncanny ability to empathize deeply with grieving families, but sometimes that emotional connection can become overwhelming. I realized that I needed to create some emotional distance. So, I started reminding myself that I was a support system, not a sponge. That mindset shift helped me provide compassionate care while still protecting my own emotional stability.

And let me tell you, seeking support from my fellow morticians and mental health professionals was a game-changer. We all go through traumatic events in this line of work, so having a network of peers who understand our unique challenges is crucial. We'd share our experiences, lend an ear, and process our emotions together. It was healing, to say the least. And those mental health professionals? They provided a safe space for me to explore my own emotions and develop healthy coping mechanisms.

Now, I won't lie to you. This journey of setting boundaries and prioritizing your emotional well-being isn't a walk in the park. It takes courage, self-reflection, and a willingness to let go of the need to be everything for everyone. But let me tell you, the rewards are immeasurable. When we protect ourselves from emotional exhaustion, we become better equipped to serve our grieving families with compassion, empathy, and professionalism. Our self-care and emotional boundaries allow us to show up as the best version of ourselves during the most difficult times in others' lives.

I hope these experiences offer you solace and let you know that you're not alone. Taking care of yourself? It's not a sign of weakness, no way. It's a sign of strength, my friend.

Because at the end of the day, the most effective way to help others is to help ourselves first.

Maintaining Work-Life Balance: Carving Out Time for Yourself

AS A MORTICIAN, LIFE can get pretty intense. It's like we're on call 24/7, constantly hustling and juggling work and personal life. Sometimes, it feels like we're drowning in our own schedules. But guess what? I've figured out the secret sauce to taking back control of my time and taking care of myself. So, buckle up and join me on this wild journey of embracing the beauty of solitude.

There's an insane tranquility that comes from being alone. It's in those rare moments of solitude that we find peace, get in touch with our thoughts, and rediscover who we truly are. But let me tell you, it's tough to separate ourselves from the emotional rollercoaster of our work in this profession. We have to figure out a way to let go and find inner peace amidst the chaos.

For me, it starts with creating a safe space in my home. I've got this cozy little corner where I can escape the madness and just revel in the beauty of my own company. It's got everything that brings me joy and instantly relaxes me. A scented candle flickers, casting hypnotic shadows on the walls. Books are stacked on shelves, ready to transport me to different worlds. And there's this comfy armchair that screams, "Curl up with a cuppa and a good book!" This little sanctuary becomes my escape, where time stands still and the world outside fades away. There is nothing in my corner that reminds me of the funeral home. It's a space where I can be me.

In our line of work, odd hours and long shifts are the name of the game. But we gotta find ways to have some me time, no matter what. For me, it means waking up early in the darkness before the craziness takes over. Everything's quiet, and there's this serene energy in the air. The sun slowly rises, painting the sky in the most glorious shades of pink and gold. I just sit there, in complete silence, watching nature wake up, being fully present in that moment. This simple act sets the tone for a mindful and intentional day ahead.

To truly embrace solitude, we need to unplug from the noise of the outside world. Our job exposes us to so much pain and suffering, it's essential to set boundaries and protect our mental well-being. That means saying goodbye to social media, turning off the never-ending notifications on our phones, and finding ways to disconnect from the constant onslaught of information. We need to allow ourselves to enjoy some quiet time, to be in touch with our thoughts and emotions without any interruptions.

But solitude doesn't mean you become a hermit. It's important to maintain connections with loved ones and have a kickass support system that understands our unique profession. That might mean scheduling regular hangouts with friends, diving headfirst into hobbies that light a fire in our souls, or simply cherishing our precious time with family. These moments of connection remind us that we're not alone in this crazy journey, that there are people who get us and have our backs.

Finding balance in our line of work is an ongoing battle, my friends. It takes constant self-reflection and evaluation. We need to regularly assess our priorities and make choices that align with our values and well-being. Sometimes, that means saying no to extra work gigs that eat into our personal time and energy. Other times, we gotta set crystal-clear boundaries with colleagues and clients, making it known when and how they can reach us outside of work. By taking back control of our schedules and setting boundaries, we carve out space for ourselves and reclaim our time.

At the end of the day, embracing solitude isn't about escaping our responsibilities or turning our backs on our work. It's about finding moments to breathe in the midst of the chaos, taking care of ourselves so we can keep being compassionate and kickass in our profession. It's about understanding that self-care is the foundation of our ability to navigate the intense emotions and demands we face. So my fellow morticians, let's make time for ourselves, embrace solitude's beauty, and nourish our souls against the storm of this demanding profession.

Building a Support Network: The Power of Connection

AS I STAND ON THE EDGE of my mortuary career, memories come flooding back of the isolation and heavy burdens that used to weigh me down. The nights felt never-ending, devoid of any comfort in the face of death. The loneliness in such an emotionally charged environment was suffocating. But it was on one particularly tough day that I realized I needed support, a tribe of people who understood the profound impact of caring for the deceased and supporting grieving families.

And so, fate intervened when I attended a professional conference. There, I met Lydia, a mortician from a nearby town. With a warm smile and a genuine desire to connect, Lydia reached out to me. She understood the untold struggles and the unspoken camaraderie that united us in our calling. Over cups of coffee and exchanged stories, we found solace in one another's experiences, as if a weight had been lifted. We became each other's rocks, companions in the otherwise solitary world of mortuary work.

The transformation that followed, both professionally and personally, was truly remarkable. The challenges that once seemed insurmountable became more bearable as the grief and stress were shared among friends who truly understood our unique work. Through the power of connection, I found comfort in the company of others who faced the same obstacles and reminded me that I wasn't alone.

In a profession where compassion fatigue looms menacingly, seeking support from those who understand our unique demands is vital for our well-being. But the question is: how do we begin to cultivate these meaningful relationships within the mortuary community?

The first step is immersing ourselves in professional organizations and conferences. Approaching these events with an open mind and a readiness to connect and share experiences is crucial. Engaging in conversations and networking with fellow morticians not only helps create friendships, but also opens doors to invaluable resources, support systems, and knowledge.

We can't forget the power of social media platforms, which have become lifelines for many professions, and ours should be no exception. Joining online groups and forums where morticians come together to discuss their daily challenges and seek advice can be a game-changer. These virtual spaces have the incredible ability to connect us with people from various backgrounds, experiences, and even different parts of the world, expanding our support network far beyond our immediate reach.

Another effective way to build connections is by volunteering in community outreach programs and grief support groups. These environments not only provide solace to grieving families, but also offer opportunities to connect with other professionals in the mortuary field. By engaging in meaningful work together, we can forge bonds and create a united front against the emotional toll our vocation can take.

While seeking support and connection is vital, it's equally important to reciprocate by being there for others. Showing compassion, lending an ear, and offering guidance to fellow morticians strengthens our network. The power of our community lies not only in receiving support but also in giving it unconditionally. By standing together, we create a robust ecosystem of care and empathy that sustains us all.

Our profession demands that we navigate the depths of grief, death, and compassion fatigue. However, by building a support network, we can unleash the transformative power of connection. Through shared experiences, understanding, and empathy, we find solace, strength, and renewed passion for our work. So let's make the effort to cultivate meaningful relationships, seek support, and embrace the transformative power of connecting with like-minded individuals who truly comprehend the unique demands and pressures we face as morticians. Together, we can conquer the challenging journey of our profession, emerging not only stronger but also with hearts filled with compassion and solidarity.

Cultivating Resilience: Thriving in the Face of Adversity

WHEN I FIRST STEPPED foot into the world of mortuary work, the pressure to provide comfort and closure to grieving families? I wasn't prepared for that. Talk about a weight on your shoulders. It's like you're expected to have all the answers, to be the shoulder to cry on, to help people make sense of the unimaginable. No pressure, right?

Here's the thing, though. Over time, I've come to realize that resilience isn't some secret superpower. It's not just reserved for those few lucky souls who were born with it. It's something you can actually develop and strengthen, like a muscle. Who woulda thought?

One of the keys to building resilience is embracing vulnerability. We morticians, we've been trained to keep our emotions locked up tight. We have this idea that vulnerability is a sign of weakness. But I've learned that it's quite the opposite. Letting ourselves be vulnerable is a sign of strength. It's about being real, raw, and open. It's about acknowledging that this job ain't easy, that it takes a toll on us, and that it's okay to feel it all. Because when we let ourselves feel, we're able to truly understand and support those who are grieving.

Another thing: self-compassion. It's easy to forget about ourselves when we're constantly taking care of others. But we gotta remember that we can't pour from an empty cup. We have to prioritize our own well-being. That means setting boundaries, asking for help when we need it, and giving ourselves permission to rest and recharge. We're not robots, after all. We're humans with feelings and limits.

And speaking of humans, community and connection are vital to resilience. We need to find our people, those who get it, who understand the unique challenges of our profession. They're the ones who lift us up when we're down, who listen without judgment, and who remind us that we're not alone in this crazy journey.

But let's not forget about self-reflection and gratitude. Taking the time to look within, to process our experiences, and to find meaning and purpose in our work? That's where the magic happens. When we reflect, we gain insight into our strengths and areas for growth. And gratitude? It helps us appreciate the little moments that make this job worthwhile, even when times get tough.

Now, I'm not saying resilience is a magic pill that solves all our problems. We still gotta take care of ourselves, you know? We need to engage in activities that bring us joy, that help us destress. Hobbies, exercise, nature - whatever floats your boat. Without taking care of ourselves, we won't have the strength to keep showing up for others.

So, my fellow morticians, let's take on this resilience journey together. Let's embrace vulnerability, practice self-compassion, seek support, reflect, and take care of ourselves. It won't be easy, but we're a tough bunch. We've got what it takes to overcome the challenges and thrive in the face of the unimaginable. Let's do this.

Emotional Resilience: Building Inner Strength

The Storm Within

Listen, let me tell you about the rollercoaster ride that is being a mortician. It's like this raging storm that stirs up emotions inside me, threatening to drown me in a sea of feelings. The sorrow and grief I see every day, it's like a weight pressing down on my heart and mind. It's heavy, man, and sometimes it feels like it's gonna crush me. But here's the thing, even in the darkness, there are these moments of light that catch you off guard.

Now, let me tell you, the toughest part of this gig is dealing with sadness. I mean, it's not your regular kind of sadness, it seeps into every fiber of your being. When you see the pain and despair etched on the faces of grieving families, it hits you hard. Some days, it feels like you're carrying the weight of the world on your shoulders. You gotta hold it together while being there for people who are going through unimaginable pain.

But, man, in the midst of all that sadness, there are these little moments of unexpected joy. It's like a memory shared, a genuine thank you, or even a smile through tears. They hit you in the gut, you know? They're bittersweet, but they bring a ray of sunshine to the darkest of days. In those moments, I see how privileged I am to do this job, to bring comfort and solace when people need it the most.

The storm inside isn't just sadness and joy. It's this wild mix of emotions that mess with your head. Guilt, for instance, is this heavy burden that sits on your chest. You wonder if you've done enough, said enough, felt enough to show that you care. Guilt whispers in your ear, making you doubt your role and questioning whether you measure up.

And then there's self-doubt. Man, it's a constant companion. Can I handle this emotionally demanding job? Will I find the strength to support those who are grieving? These doubts gnaw at you, shaking your confidence and making you question your purpose. It takes some serious soul-searching and resilience to fight against these doubts, to remind yourself of the impact you have on people's lives.

Finding peace in the midst of this storm ain't no easy task, let me tell you. It takes a lot of self-awareness, self-compassion, and making yourself a priority. One thing that's helped me is accepting my limitations. I've learned that I can't fix everything, and that's okay. My job is to create a safe space for healing, not to play the hero.

I've also found solace in reaching out to others who understand this crazy profession. Support groups, therapy, and just hanging out with colleagues who get it, it's been a lifesaver. Sharing our stories and talking about our experiences, it's like a lifeline. It reminds me that I'm not alone in this storm.

Imagine this: you find yourself in a room filled with like-minded professionals, each sharing insights into the ever-evolving landscape of mortuary science. This isn't just another networking event; it's a workshop, a seminar, a place where knowledge is not only gained but also exchanged. Engaging in continuous education is akin to opening a window in a stuffy room; suddenly, fresh perspectives and new ideas waft in. As a mortician, actively seeking out these opportunities not only keeps you abreast of the latest industry trends but also imparts a sense of competence.

Continuous education isn't just about attending workshops; it's about the pursuit of specialization. Picture yourself delving into a niche within mortuary science that resonates with your passion. Whether it's the art of embalming, the intricacies of funeral planning, or the evolving landscape of grief counseling, becoming an expert in a particular field can be a powerful antidote to self-doubt. As you acquire specialized knowledge, you not only deepen your expertise but also foster a sense of mastery and confidence in your abilities.

Online courses offer a flexible avenue for learning, allowing you to enhance your skills at your own pace and from the comfort of your own space. The virtual realm becomes a classroom, offering a plethora of resources to bolster your professional arsenal. Imagine the empowerment that comes with acquiring a new skill or mastering a cutting-edge technique—all at your fingertips.

Then there's the magic of networking. Picture a virtual or physical space where morticians from diverse backgrounds converge to share experiences, challenges, and triumphs. Building connections within the industry creates a support system that can be invaluable in moments of self-doubt. Learning from the experiences of others, whether through formal mentorship or casual conversations, adds layers of insight to your professional journey.

Now, let's shift our focus to reflecting on success—an art often overlooked but essential in cultivating confidence. Imagine creating a journal—a tangible record of your triumphs. In moments of doubt, this journal becomes a trove of positivity, reminding you of successful arrangements, moments of genuine connection with grieving families, and instances where your expertise shone through.

Setting and celebrating goals becomes another brushstroke in your confidence canvas. Picture the satisfaction that comes with achieving both short-term and long-term objectives. Each accomplishment, no matter how small, becomes a beacon of reassurance in the storm of self-doubt.

Client testimonials take on a special significance. Imagine reading heartfelt expressions of gratitude from families you've served during their most vulnerable moments. These testimonials aren't just words; they are affirmations of your impact, reminders that you've made a positive difference in the lives of others.

Performance reviews, often viewed with trepidation, transform into opportunities for self-reflection. Instead of fixating on perceived shortcomings, focus on areas where you've excelled. Use constructive feedback not as a source of self-doubt but as a roadmap for continuous improvement.

Sharing success stories during team meetings or casual conversations becomes a communal celebration. Your victories inspire others, creating a positive work environment where everyone's achievements are acknowledged and celebrated.

Creating a professional portfolio is akin to assembling a gallery of your accomplishments. Imagine flipping through pages that showcase your projects, skills, and growth over time. It becomes a visual testament to your journey, reinforcing your competence and providing a tangible source of pride.

In the quiet moments, engage in self-appraisal. Picture yourself taking stock of your own performance, identifying areas of excellence and instances where you've triumphed over challenges. This introspection isn't a mere exercise; it's a deliberate act of recognizing your strengths and building confidence from within.

In the symphony of mortuary practice, continuous education and reflecting on success harmonize to create a melody of confidence. It's a journey—a dynamic dance where learning and self-reflection become partners, guiding morticians through the ebb and flow of their professional lives. As you embrace these allies, self-doubt retreats, making space for the crescendo of confidence to resonate within you.

Let me tell you, my friend, self-care is where it's at. Taking time for yourself, engaging in activities that nourish your mind, body, and spirit, that's essential. Whether it's your hobbies, meditation, or just taking a walk in nature, those small acts of self-care make a world of difference. They fill your compassion tank and give you the strength to keep going.

This storm within, man, it's a part of being a mortician. It's a reminder of our shared humanity, the bonds we form through both sorrow and joy. It's through this storm that we discover our capacity to hold space for others and our strength to weather any emotional tempest. So, my friend, if you're in this profession, embrace the storm, find your inner calm, and keep on navigating these choppy waters with grace, compassion, and resilience. You got this.

The Mask We Wear

YOU KNOW, BEING A MORTICIAN is not as straightforward as it seems. It's like we're playing two roles at once - one as our true selves, and the other as the unflinching pillars of support for grieving families. It's a delicate balancing act, really.

I mean, when people think of masks in our line of work, they usually picture the physical ones we wear in the embalming room or when things get tough. And let me tell you, those masks are a blessing. They shield our faces from the unsettling sights we come across and help us focus on the task at hand without getting overwhelmed by raw emotions.

But the real mask we wear is the one that hides our vulnerability and keeps our composure intact. Society expects us to be strong and unshakeable, even when we're crumbling inside. We have to be the constant in a sea of grief, offering solace and stability to those in their darkest moments.

However, this mask we wear takes a toll on us. It can be emotionally draining to suppress our own feelings while carrying the weight of others' sorrow. We find ourselves caught in a struggle, our hearts breaking for the families we serve while unable to fully express our own grief.

It's called compassion fatigue, you know - this state of exhaustion that comes from constantly being there for others, even when we're running on empty. The daily exposure to death and grieving families chips away at our emotional well-being, making us feel detached and depleted. It's a tough balancing act, trying to be there for others while taking care of ourselves.

So, how do you overcome compassion fatigue? Let's explore some friendly and practical steps.

First and foremost, imagine giving yourself permission to acknowledge your feelings. Compassion fatigue doesn't mean you lack empathy or care—it's a sign that you've been consistently giving your heart to others. Begin by recognizing that it's okay to feel the weight of your work; you're not alone in this sentiment.

Consider creating a sanctuary for your emotions. Picture a space, be it physical or metaphorical, where you can retreat and recharge. It could be a quiet corner in your home, a serene outdoor spot, or even a few moments of meditation. This sanctuary becomes a refuge—a place to process emotions, reflect, and rejuvenate.

Now, envision the power of setting boundaries. Picture yourself establishing clear limits on the emotional energy you invest in each situation. Understand that while empathy is your superpower, it's essential to conserve some of that energy for your own well-being. It's not about distancing yourself; it's about creating a healthy balance.

Imagine incorporating self-care rituals into your routine. Picture moments of indulgence—whether it's a warm bath, a good book, or a hobby that brings you joy. These rituals are not indulgences; they are necessities, vital to replenishing your emotional reserves.

Seek out a support system. Picture a network of friends, family, or colleagues who understand the unique challenges of your profession. Share your experiences, not as a burden, but as a way to lighten your emotional load. Knowing that you're not alone in your journey can be incredibly comforting.

Consider the transformative power of professional supervision or counseling. Picture a safe space where you can openly discuss your experiences with someone trained to guide you through the complexities of compassion fatigue. It's not a sign of weakness to seek support; it's a courageous step toward healing.

Now, let's explore the magic of gratitude. Picture yourself actively acknowledging the positive aspects of your work. It could be a heartfelt thank-you from a family, a shared moment of solace, or the knowledge that you've made a meaningful impact. Cultivating gratitude can be a potent antidote to the emotional toll of compassion fatigue.

Imagine integrating regular breaks into your schedule. Picture moments of respite during your workday—short pauses to step outside, take a few deep breaths, or engage in a brief mindfulness exercise. These pauses become small but significant anchors, grounding you in the present moment.

Last, picture the strength that comes from seeking variety in your work. If possible, consider rotating through different aspects of mortuary practice. This variety not only enhances your skills but also prevents emotional burnout by introducing fresh perspectives and challenges.

In the tapestry of mortuary practice, compassion fatigue is a thread woven into the fabric of caring deeply. By envisioning these steps—acknowledging, creating sanctuaries, setting boundaries, practicing self-care, seeking support, fostering gratitude, embracing breaks, and introducing variety—you can mend that thread. Overcoming compassion fatigue is not about diminishing your compassion; it's about nurturing it in a way that ensures your light continues to shine brightly, both for yourself and the families you serve.

Mindfulness and meditation do wonders as well. By taking a moment to be present and reflect, we can peel back the layers of our emotional masks and truly connect with ourselves. Mindful breathing and self-reflection create a space where our emotions can freely flow, helping us heal and find some sort of balance in our role as morticians.

And let's not forget about rituals. Incorporating some sort of meaningful ritual into our daily lives can bring a sense of closure and purpose. It's a way to honor the lives we touch, acknowledge our experiences, and release our emotions in a structured and intentional manner. Whether it's a simple act like lighting a candle or a more elaborate ceremony, these practices can help us find healing and closure.

But here's the thing we need to remember - wearing a mask doesn't make us any less human. It's just a tool we use to navigate the complexities and challenges of our profession. It's important to find a way to safely remove those masks, allowing ourselves to be vulnerable and authentic. That's when we can truly provide compassionate care for the families we serve and nurture our own well-being.

In our quest for authenticity, we need to be gentle with ourselves. It's okay to feel a whole range of emotions, even in the midst of grief. Our vulnerability doesn't make us less professional - if anything, it enhances our ability to connect with others on a deeper level. By embracing our true selves, masks and all, we can find emotional release, reclaim our humanity, and continue serving our communities with compassion, empathy, and resilience.

The Dance of Empathy

I GOTTA TELL YOU, UNDERSTANDING empathy in the mortuary profession is like trying to learn a complicated dance routine. It's like you have to put yourself in someone else's shoes and really feel what they're feeling. Sympathy just ain't enough, my friend. We gotta really connect with these grieving families and be there for them in a whole new way.

But let me tell you, this dance of empathy isn't as easy as it sounds. We gotta tread carefully, or we risk running ourselves into the ground. I'm talking about something called compassion fatigue, or secondary traumatic stress. It's when we absorb all the emotional suffering of others and it starts to mess with our own well-being. And let me tell you, as morticians, we see grief and loss on a regular basis. If we're not careful, it can take a huge toll on our mental and emotional health.

So here's the thing - we gotta find that balance, you know? We gotta be there for these families, but we also gotta take care of ourselves. One way we can do that is by really listening to what these families are saying. When we actively listen, we show them that we get it. We show them that we care. And that builds trust, my friend. Trust that lets us be there for them in the ways they need.

Now, setting emotional boundaries is key. I mean, we gotta remember that we're professionals, right? We gotta protect ourselves from getting overwhelmed by all the emotions flying around. It's all about knowing our limits and finding ways to take care of ourselves. We gotta take breaks, do things that bring us joy, and reach out for support when we need it.

Picture this: you, as a mortician, navigate the intricate dance of feeling deeply for the families you serve while also safeguarding your own emotional well-being. How do you maintain the warmth of empathy without succumbing to its potential overwhelm? Let's explore this delicate dance with a friendly and practical guide.

First, imagine embracing the superpower of empathy. Picture yourself fully present with grieving families, offering a listening ear and a compassionate heart. Empathy is the thread that weaves genuine connections—it's the ability to understand and share the feelings of others. Celebrate this gift, for it forms the foundation of the support you provide.

Now, let's envision the importance of setting emotional boundaries. Picture a protective bubble around your emotional core, a shield that allows you to be compassionate without absorbing the weight of others' emotions. This boundary isn't about shutting off; it's about creating a safe space for both you and the families you serve.

Consider the power of active listening. Picture yourself fully engaged in the stories and emotions shared by grieving families. Listening not only deepens your understanding but also allows you to connect on a profound level. It's a two-way street where empathy flows naturally.

Imagine the strength that comes from recognizing your own emotional limits. Picture yourself tuning into your feelings and acknowledging when you need a moment to recalibrate. This self-awareness is a cornerstone of maintaining emotional well-being while being a pillar of support for others.

Envision the practice of compartmentalization as a skillful tool. Picture yourself mentally putting emotions into separate boxes—acknowledging them but not letting them intertwine. This allows you to be present with families in the moment while preserving your emotional equilibrium.

Now, let's explore the magic of self-compassion. Picture yourself treating your own emotions with the same kindness you extend to others. Understand that it's okay to feel deeply and, at times, be affected by the profound experiences you encounter. Self-compassion becomes a nurturing balm for your own emotional landscape.

Consider the transformative power of reflection. Picture yourself taking moments to process your emotions after particularly challenging situations. Reflecting allows you to learn from experiences, reinforcing your emotional resilience and fortifying your empathetic capabilities.

Imagine the art of communicating effectively. Picture yourself expressing your own needs to colleagues or supervisors when necessary. Open communication ensures that you're supported in maintaining your emotional balance, fostering a collaborative and understanding work environment.

Last, picture the beauty of seeking support when needed. Imagine turning to friends, family, or professional mentors to share your experiences and feelings. This support network becomes a source of strength, reminding you that you're not alone in navigating the delicate interplay of empathy and emotional boundaries.

In the compassionate tapestry of mortuary practice, empathy and emotional boundaries dance hand in hand. By envisioning these steps—celebrating empathy, setting protective boundaries, active listening, recognizing limits, practicing compartmentalization, embracing self-compassion, reflecting, communicating effectively, and seeking support—you not only honor the connections you forge with families but also safeguard the precious flame of your own emotional well-being. It's a harmonious dance that allows you to be both a beacon of support and a guardian of your own heart.

And don't even get me started on self-care. It's not just a buzzword, my friend. It's crucial. Taking care of ourselves lets us be there for these families in the best way possible. We gotta exercise, meditate, spend time with loved ones, and do things we love. That's how we build up our emotional resilience, my friend.

But hey, let's not ignore the signs of compassion fatigue. If we're feeling emotionally exhausted, cranky, can't sleep, or can't feel empathy anymore, we gotta ask for help. There's no shame in it, my friend. It's a sign of our commitment to giving the best care we can.

This dance of empathy in the mortuary profession is no joke. It's challenging, but it's also incredibly rewarding. When we can be there for these grieving families during their darkest moments, when we can create a safe space for them to heal, that's when we know we're doing something right. We just can't forget to take care of ourselves along the way.

Being a mortician is more than just a job. It's a calling, a responsibility. We're there for people at their most vulnerable, helping them through the unimaginable pain of losing a loved one. And believe me, it's a delicate dance we're doing. We've gotta be in tune with their emotions, but also protect ourselves from getting overwhelmed.

This dance of empathy is all about being present, being connected. It's about really feeling the pain of others, and standing beside them as they face their heartbreak. We listen to their stories, their memories, their pain, and we carry it with us in our hearts.

But let me tell you, this dance ain't without its risks. If we're not careful, the weight of grief can drag us down. Compassion fatigue can creep in, making it harder for us to offer genuine support. So we gotta know our boundaries, protect ourselves from getting too caught up.

But there's hope, my friend. It's all about self-awareness, self-love. Active listening becomes our guide, helping us understand and support these grieving families. And setting emotional boundaries? It's a necessity. We gotta remember that we're professionals, taking care of the living and honoring the departed.

Self-care is the solid foundation of this dance. It's what keeps us going, what keeps our empathy alive. We gotta do things that bring us joy, that fill our souls. It's how we stay emotionally strong, how we can keep giving.

But even with all our efforts, there may be times when we stumble. That's when we gotta recognize the signs and reach out for help. Therapy, support groups, trusted colleagues - they can all be our lifelines. We gotta take care of ourselves to keep taking care of others.

This dance of empathy in the mortuary profession is a testament to our dedication and compassion. We're there to offer a helping hand, to provide comfort and support. And it's not an easy dance, my friend. It takes strength, resilience, and a commitment to others. So let's keep dancing, one step at a time.

Cultivating Resilience

YOU KNOW, ONE OF THE first things we gotta do to tough it out in this profession is to really acknowledge and give credit to our own damn emotions. I mean, let's face it, we're constantly surrounded by grief and loss, and it's so damn easy to just shut off and become numb to our own feelings. But trust me, it's hella important to recognize and validate what we're going through, and give ourselves a chance to process and heal. I mean, we gotta find ways to let it out, ya know? Maybe through writing in a journal, creating some art, or just talking it out with a buddy or therapist who's got our back.

And yeah, speaking of taking care of ourselves, self-care is not just some fancy luxury – it's freakin' necessary for our well-being. We need to make ourselves a priority, both physically and emotionally. That means doing things that make us happy and relaxed, like getting our sweat on through exercise, meditating our troubles away, or just chillin' out in nature. We also need to know when to set some boundaries and say "hell no" when we're being pulled in too many directions. 'Cause let me tell ya, trying to please everyone and overdoing it will just lead to burnout, and that's the last thing we need if we wanna stay strong and resilient.

Now, building a support network is another key move in this resilience game. Let's be real, our line of work can get pretty damn lonely. We're constantly carrying the weight of other people's grief on our shoulders, day in and day out. But reaching out to others who understand our struggles can make a world of difference. I'm talking about joining professional groups or finding a support group specifically for folks like us. Having regular chats with colleagues who are going through the same crap can really make us feel less alone. Plus, they might even have some insights or tips that'll help us out, you know?

But there's one thing that always gets me fired up and reminds me why I love this crazy job – gaining a bigger perspective. It's so easy to get caught up in the daily grind and stress, but if we take a step back and think about the impact we have – wow, it can really light a fire in our hearts. Just think about it – we're providing comfort and closure to people in their darkest times. We're the ones who help 'em find some peace when everything's falling apart. So let that sink in, my friend, and remember just how damn important our role is in all of this.

And hey, don't forget about personal and professional growth. We can't stay stuck in the same damn place forever. We gotta keep learning and growing with the times. That means keeping up with new techniques and trends in our field, and maybe even taking some classes or workshops. It's all about adapting and being ready for whatever gets thrown our way. And let me tell you, being prepared and confident in tough situations, that's a big part of staying resilient.

Last but definitely not least, we gotta show ourselves some damn compassion. Yeah, we're caretakers by nature, but that doesn't mean we forget about our own well-being. We're human too, damn it. We're gonna feel the emotional weight of our work, and that's okay. So be gentle with yourself, cut yourself some slack, and know that it's normal to make mistakes and learn from 'em. And don't forget to celebrate your strengths and accomplishments, no matter how tiny they may seem in the face of all the hardship.

So there you have it, my friend – resilience ain't something we're just born with or without. It's a skill that we can freakin' cultivate and strengthen over time. By taking care of ourselves, building a support network, gaining a bigger perspective, seeking growth opportunities, and showing ourselves some love and compassion, we can tap into that badass resilience within us. So buckle up, my friend, 'cause with resilience on our side, we'll navigate this wild journey in the mortuary profession with strength and grace.

Finding Light in the Darkness

I REMEMBER THIS ONE funeral that will forever be etched in my mind. It was for this young boy, couldn't have been more than 13 years old, whose life was tragically cut short. As I stood there, surrounded by tear-stained faces and hushed whispers, the weight of everyone's grief felt almost suffocating. My heart shattered into a million pieces.

We were a community mourning the loss of an innocent soul gone too soon. Parents should never have to bury their children. It just didn't seem fair or right. Waves of sorrow flooded the room as loved ones struggled to process this nightmarish tragedy. I saw raw anguish in every red, puffy eye.

In times like these, it's tempting to shut down emotionally, to protect our hearts from the threat of complete devastation.

But the shared experience of pain also has an incredible power to unite us. As I gazed upon the boy's serene face at the front of the room, I realized we were all connected in this profound moment of grief. It gently reminded me that even the darkest tragedies can bring light and meaning over time.

Our line of work opens the door to the most difficult and intimate spaces between life and death. We bear witness to the messiest, most painful corners of the human experience. As heavy as that responsibility feels, it also makes me appreciate the fragility and sanctity of each life. When I methodically clean, dress and prepare a body for its final farewell, showing care and respect for both the deceased and the bereaved, I am shining a small light in the darkness for those left behind.

There have been many times when the crushing weight of sorrow threatens to extinguish my own inner light. But the incredible resilience of the human spirit always manages to reignite that flame. During one unforgettable funeral for a devoted mother taken too soon by cancer, I watched her heartbroken family transform from faces flooded with anguish to faces glowing with nostalgic joy as they swapped stories about her vibrant spirit. Even in life's bleakest moments, the light finds a way to creep back in, reminding us of love's eternal glow.

You know, it's not just in the lives of the deceased that we find these moments of light. We experience it ourselves as morticians. We see the incredible strength and resilience of the human spirit, and that's what keeps us going. We gotta embrace that light in the darkness, recognize the impact we have on others, and find hope in all the sorrow. That's how we take care of ourselves and handle the stress and compassion fatigue that come with our noble work.

As morticians, we've chosen a path that takes us right into the heart of grief. But let me tell you, it's within that darkness that we find the most growth and transformation. Even in the darkest moments, there's always a glimmer of light, and it's up to us to hold onto it. Let it guide us through the shadows and remind us of the profound impact we have on people's lives.

Physical Self-Care: Nurturing the Body

The Ritual of Morning Stretching

Imagine waking up each morning to the soft glow of dawn, its delicate light peeking through your bedroom window like a gentle caress. You reluctantly peel yourself away from the comfort of your bed, feeling the weight of yesterday's exhaustion still clinging to your weary muscles. As you shuffle towards a tranquil corner of your home, you take a moment to gather your thoughts, mentally preparing for the challenges that lie ahead. This morning ritual has become your secret weapon, an armor of sorts, helping you navigate the treacherous terrain of both physical and emotional obstacles that await you.

With each languorous stretch, you can feel the tension in your body slowly dissipating. You inhale deeply, raising your arms overhead, your spine elongating as if reaching towards the heavens. Your chest expands, as if embracing the promise of a brand new day. And as you exhale, your arms gracefully descend, folding yourself forward, releasing the burdens and worries that have nestled themselves within your soul. With each gentle movement, the juxtaposition of effort and surrender creates a delicate dance, a symphony of release and rebirth.

The subsequent stretch leads you into a tranquil twist. With one hand lightly resting on the opposite knee, you rotate your torso, feeling your dormant muscles stirring to life. With each revolution, you free the shackles of stagnant energy that have weighed you down, creating a fertile ground for new experiences and fresh beginnings. Your body becomes a vessel, a conduit for both release and revival, as you surrender to the rhythmic flow of movement that cleanses your spirit and rejuvenates your entire being.

As your morning stretching routine unfolds, you transition to a series of gentle lunges, gracefully opening and stretching your hips. Each deliberate step not only awakens your dormant muscles, but also anchors you firmly to the present moment, like roots burrowing deep into the rich soil of the earth. The rhythmic synchronization of breath and motion transports you into a state of mindfulness, a heightened awareness of the sensations pulsating through your body. You can feel the energy coursing through your veins, invigorating both your mind and body, preparing you to face the demanding tasks that lay ahead with a renewed sense of purpose.

The final act of your morning stretching ritual finds you seated, your legs extended before you. As you reach forward, a pleasant stretch engulfs your hamstrings, like the gentle unfolding of a beautiful secret. In this moment of tranquility, you pause to reflect on the intentions that will guide your steps throughout the day. Compassion and care become your sacred mantras, as you remind yourself of the profound importance of your role as a mortician. In the silence of this contemplative pause, you reconnect with your purpose, reaffirming your unwavering commitment to serving others.

Through each deliberate stretch and movement, your senses awaken. The unhurried ebb and flow of your stretching routine not only nourishes your physical body, but also paints vibrant strokes of colors onto the canvas of your mind and soul. It becomes a sanctuary, a sacred practice of self-care and introspection before you step into the realm of caring for others.

By incorporating this simple yet profound practice into your daily routine, you have the power to transform your well-being as a mortician. It serves as a conduit to release physical tension and cultivate emotional resilience. The mindful fusion of movement and breath taps into wellsprings of inner strength, allowing you to find equilibrium amidst the oftentimes trying circumstances you face.

As you embark on this new day, remember the gentle necessity of tending to your own needs. Embrace the ritual of morning stretching, infusing it with the duality of self-care and compassion. As you bid farewell to the burdens of yesteryears, you create a vast space for the tender care and compassion you are poised to offer. By honoring your body, awakening your senses, and invigorating your mind, you set the stage for a day infused with resilience, mindfulness, and an unwavering ability to discover beauty in both life and death.

Fueling Your Body: Nourishing Nutrition

YOU KNOW, BEING A MORTICIAN ain't no walk in the park. Every day is filled with grief and the weight of the departed weighing down on us. It's hard to find time for ourselves when we're busy taking care of others. But you know what? Taking care of our own bodies is just as important as tending to the deceased. It's like when we meticulously prepare the bodies for their final resting place, we should give that same level of care and attention to our own well-being.

Picture this: a plate overflowing with vibrant, colorful fruits and veggies. I'm talking about a feast for the senses here. It's not just pleasing to look at, but it's a reminder of the energy and vitality these foods give us. Our bodies deserve to be nourished and cared for just like we care for those who have passed.

When we chow down on nutrient-packed foods, we're arming our bodies with what they need to fight off stress and fatigue. You ever notice how chicken, fish, and legumes give us energy that lasts? That's because they're packed with amino acids and other goodies that repair tissue and keep everything running smoothly. It's like a slow and steady release of fuel to keep us going, even when we're dealing with all sorts of emotional chaos.

And let's not forget about those whole grains, like quinoa and whole wheat bread. These guys are the secret sauce to a balanced diet. They're full of fiber and they give us a steady supply of energy, so we don't crash and burn like a car with no gas. Plus, that fiber keeps our digestion in check and helps us stay full for longer. You can't put a price on that, especially during those long nights where we're taking care of grieving families and the deceased.

But it's not just about the physical benefits. It's about our emotions too. Mindful eating is all about taking a moment to appreciate the food we're putting in our mouths. It's about slowing down and savoring the flavors, so we don't just mindlessly stuff our faces. Being present when we eat is a game-changer, especially when our lives are on autopilot most of the time.

Creating balanced meals isn't as hard as it seems. It actually feels like an act of self-care, you know? Taking time to plan and prepare our meals gives us a chance to reclaim our personal time and put our nutrition first. Maybe for you, chopping veggies or cooking up a meal after a long day is therapeutic. It's a way to recharge and feel a sense of control amidst the craziness of our work.

We've gotta pay attention to how our bodies react to different foods too. How do we feel after we chow down? Are certain foods leaving us feeling sluggish and bloated? While others give us a burst of energy and mental clarity? These little indicators help us figure out what works best for our bodies and what doesn't. It's like we're on a quest to find the perfect balance of nourishment.

I get it though. It's tempting to grab something quick and convenient when we're knee-deep in work. But when we make a conscious effort to prioritize our well-being, it's like a superpower. We can serve others with more effectiveness and compassion when we're fueled by nourishing, wholesome foods. It's not just about self-care, it's about having the energy and vitality to honor the departed and continue our sacred work.

So, let's go on this culinary adventure together, my friend. Let's discover the power of nutrient-packed foods that give our bodies the sustenance and nourishment they crave. As we embark on this mindful eating journey, may we find strength, resilience, and comfort in each and every bite. Because when we take care of ourselves, we can continue to uphold the legacy of compassion that defines our noble profession.

The Dance of Self-Care: Finding Joy in Movement

BEING A MORTICIAN, you're constantly surrounded by death and grief. It can really take a toll on you, physically, mentally, and emotionally. It's important to find ways to release all that accumulated stress and give your spirit a fresh dose of life. And for me, that's through dancing.

Dancing, my friend, is like a universal language that goes beyond words. It lets us express ourselves in ways that words just can't capture. When we dance, our bodies become vessels of emotion and release—we communicate through movement. It's a gateway to healing, a chance to rediscover who we are deep down, and it's brought me so much joy and solace.

Now, the world of dance is a vast one, my friend, offering all sorts of styles with their own unique benefits and therapeutic qualities. From the grace and elegance of ballet to the raw energy of hip-hop, there's bound to be something that speaks to your soul. So, go ahead and explore, try them all on like new identities until you find the one that gets your heart racing.

Ballet, for instance, is all about elegance and grace. As a mortician, it can be especially nurturing. The fluid movements and sweeping gestures not only train your body to move with poise and precision, but they also help you be present and mindful. In those moments on the dance floor, you can let go of the past and the future, just focusing on the here and now. Ballet brings structure and discipline into your life, something that can be a welcome escape from the emotional chaos of your work.

Now, on the complete opposite end of the spectrum, we have hip-hop. This style is all about high energy and expressing yourself. It lets you tap into that raw emotion that's been bubbling under the surface. With its strong beats and dynamic rhythms, hip-hop empowers you to release all that pent-up stress and frustration. You can turn it into vitality and creative expression. It's a way to reclaim control over your emotions and feel strong and resilient—both on and off the dance floor.

But don't you worry, my friend, dance isn't just about ballet and hip-hop. There are countless other styles waiting for you to explore. Contemporary dance with its soulful movements, salsa with its vibrant rhythms, African dance with its exuberant energy—each brings its own therapeutic benefits. The golden rule is to listen to your body and let the music guide you. Get rid of any preconceived notions and let your body's wisdom take over. Trust me, it knows how to move and express itself better than your conscious mind ever could.

As you embark on this dance journey, my friend, remember that self-care isn't just about finding joy through movement. It's about reconnecting with your authentic self and reclaiming your body. Our profession sometimes forces us to disconnect from our physicality, treating our bodies like mere tools. But dance, oh dance, it's a way for us to heal those wounds of detachment and see our bodies as sacred vessels of life once again.

In the rhythm of dance, my friend, you'll find a powerful tool for self-expression and stress relief. As you gracefully or energetically glide across that dance floor, you'll shed layers of stress and tension. It's like you're releasing the weight of the day, freeing yourself from all the chaos and pain. And in that freedom, you'll rediscover the beauty and joy that's still present in life.

Picture this: as a mortician, you step into your role not just as a practitioner but as a choreographer of compassion, utilizing the fluidity of movement and the rhythm of connection to guide you through the delicate intricacies of working with the departed and comforting grieving families.

First, envision the significance of adopting a dancer's mindset. Picture yourself approaching each interaction with a sense of artistry and mindfulness, just like a dancer on stage. In the world of dance, every movement is intentional, every step purposeful. Similarly, in mortuary practice, every action can be approached with a mindful choreography, ensuring that you navigate the space with grace and precision.

Imagine utilizing rhythm as a guiding force. Picture the rhythm of your breath as you prepare a body or engage in conversation with grieving families. By embracing the natural ebb and flow, you establish a steady tempo, allowing you to lose yourself in the choreography of the moment while remaining emotionally present. The rhythm becomes a grounding force, a reliable beat that anchors you amidst the emotional currents.

Now, let's explore the concept of losing oneself in the choreography. Picture the freedom that comes with surrendering to the dance of your responsibilities. As a mortician, you immerse yourself in the tasks at hand, allowing the muscle memory of your skills to guide you. This immersion isn't a detachment from emotion; rather, it's a way of navigating the complexities with a focused and rhythmic flow.

Envision the body as a canvas for your choreography. Picture the gentle movements and meticulous care you provide, not as mechanical tasks, but as a dance of reverence. Each touch, each gesture becomes a stroke in a beautiful composition, honoring the departed with a choreography of utmost respect.

Imagine extending this dancer's mindset to your interactions with grieving families. Picture the cadence of your words, the pacing of your conversations. By infusing a sense of rhythm into your communication, you create a comforting and harmonious space. This rhythmic dialogue becomes a dance of empathy, a choreography of support that transcends mere words.

Consider the transformative power of using dance as a means of control. Picture yourself maintaining control not through rigidity but through the fluidity of movement. In the dance of mortuary practice, control becomes a dynamic force, allowing you to guide the process with both precision and emotional finesse.

Last, picture the beauty of finding joy in the dance. As you move through the steps of your responsibilities, imagine experiencing a sense of fulfillment and purpose. The dance becomes not just a series of tasks but a celebration of life, a rhythmic ode to the stories you help preserve and the comfort you provide to grieving hearts.

In the rhythm and choreography of mortuary practice, adopting a dancer's mindset becomes a transformative journey. By envisioning these steps—embracing intentionality, utilizing rhythm, losing oneself in the choreography, treating the body as a canvas, extending the mindset to interactions, using dance as a means of control, and finding joy in the dance—you elevate your role from a mere practitioner to a compassionate choreographer, creating a dance of solace and support for both the departed and those left behind. It's a harmonious dance that unfolds with grace, precision, and emotional resonance.

So, my friend, I invite you to unleash that inner dancer within you. Embark on this journey of self-discovery through movement. Be open-minded as you explore different dance styles, and be brave in heart. It's a learning process, both an art and a form of self-care. Let the music take over, surrender to the rhythm, and let dance guide you to a deeper connection with yourself and the world around you.

In this dance of self-care, my friend, you'll find joy, solace, and renewal—all wrapped up in one beautiful package. Embrace this gift of movement, let it transform not only your practice as a mortician but your entire life. Dance will become your ally in conquering the challenges of your profession, leading you down a path of healing and self-compassion. So, step onto that dance floor and let the magic begin.

The Power of Rest: Recharging Your Batteries

YOU KNOW, I CAN'T STRESS enough just how important rest is in our lives. Trust me, as a mortician, I understand firsthand the toll our job takes on our physical and mental well-being. The long hours, the emotional drain, and constantly being surrounded by grief and sorrow can really wear us down. That's why we have got to prioritize getting some good ol' rejuvenating sleep and tap into the transformative power of rest as part of our self-care routine.

First things first, let's talk about creating a peaceful sleep environment. I'm telling you, your surroundings can make a world of difference when it comes to relaxing and unwinding. Take a look at your bedroom and ask yourself, "Does this place feel like a sanctuary, or more like a cluttered mess?" Get rid of anything that stresses you out, and instead, fill the space with things that bring you peace and comfort.

Now, let's set the mood, baby. Soft lighting is where it's at. Try adding some bedside lamps or even dimming the room lights to create a serene ambiance. And if you really want to take it to the next level, introduce some calming scents like lavender essential oil. Trust me, your nostrils will thank you. Oh, and don't forget about your mattress and pillows. Get yourself something comfortable that suits your sleep preferences. Because let's face it, the key is to make your sleep environment a place you can't wait to crawl into every night.

But hey, even in the silence of our bedrooms, sometimes our minds just won't shut up. You know what I'm talking about, right? That's when relaxation techniques come to the rescue. Meditation and deep breathing exercises are like secret weapons that can calm your mind and get you into a restful state.

Picture this: Find yourself a cozy position, close your eyes, and hone in on your breath. Inhale all that positivity and tranquility, filling up your lungs. Then on the exhale, imagine letting go of all the tension and worries that are weighing you down. Let your body just relax completely, feeling the weight of your limbs sinking deep into the bed. Keep up this deep breathing pattern as you release any racing thoughts and focus solely on your breath.

Now, if you struggle with meditation at first, don't sweat it. It takes time and practice to quiet the mind, so start with just a few minutes each night and work your way up as you get more comfortable with it.

Let me drop some knowledge on you about sleep, my friend. This isn't just some luxury we're talking about here. It's essential for our physical and mental well-being. Research has shown that lack of sleep can mess with your health in all kinds of ways, like weakening your immune system, increasing your risk of heart disease, and even making your brain less sharp.

But when we actually give our bodies the gift of enough rest, magic happens. I'm talking repair, rejuvenation, and regeneration, my friend. During those deep sleep cycles, our muscles relax, our cells get their groove back, and our immune system takes a power-up. And mentally, sleep plays a vital role in managing our mood, helping us consolidate memories, and keeping our brains sharp as a tack.

And here's where it gets good. When we prioritize restful sleep in our self-care routine, we unlock some serious potential. Imagine waking up after a peaceful night's sleep, feeling like a million bucks. Your mind is clear, your body is pumped up and ready to go, and your spirit is soaring. That's the power of quality rest right there. And when we're running on that kind of energy, we can give our absolute best to our work and to the people we serve.

So, now that we know how crucial rest is, let's figure out how to make it a non-negotiable part of our self-care routine. Start by taking a look at your current sleep habits. Are you staying up way too late getting sucked into those Netflix marathons? Is your sleep environment more like a battlefield than a sanctuary? Are there stresses and worries that are haunting you before you hit the hay? Identify what's holding you back from a good night's sleep, and make a commitment to change it.

Set yourself a regular sleep schedule that actually allows for enough hours of sleep, and stick to it like it's your new religion. And speaking of religion, create your own little bedtime ritual that tells your body and mind it's time to unwind and get ready for sleep. Maybe it's stretching, writing in a journal, or diving into a good book. Find what works for you, sister, and make it a non-negotiable part of your self-care practice.

Rest isn't just something nice to have. It's an absolute necessity for our well-being, especially for us morticians dealing with all these unique challenges. When we embrace the power of rest, we find those peaceful moments in the midst of chaos, and we come out the other side with a fresh burst of energy to keep doing the important work we do.

Remember, create that peaceful sleep environment, dive into those relaxation techniques, and understand just how massively important quality sleep is for our overall well-being. By doing these things, we show up each day with a renewed sense of energy, ready to take on the world with compassion and vitality.

So, my dear, let's take a deep dive into the power of rest and make sleep an absolute sacred part of our self-care routine. It's through that rejuvenating sleep that we can feed our bodies, heal our minds, and keep shining bright in the lives of those we serve.

Soothing the Senses: The Healing Touch

THERE'S SOMETHING TRULY magical about the simplicity of touch, ya know? Just a gentle brush of a hand, a comforting hug, or a soothing massage can work wonders on our state of mind and lift the weight off our shoulders. It's like we have this untapped power within us to heal ourselves, if only we take the time to explore it.

For me, self-massage has been a game-changer in the world of self-care. It's all about using your own hands to knead and work those tight muscles, melting away tension and inviting pure relaxation. This technique has been around for ages, and let me tell you, it hasn't lost its touch.

When you're ready to dive into the world of self-massage, set the scene, my friend. Find a quiet corner where you can escape the chaos and truly immerse yourself in the experience. Dim the lights, play some soothing tunes, and let the sweet scent of essential oils fill the air. Trust me, it's the perfect recipe for a little slice of bliss. Whether or not you believe in the healing properties of essential oils doesn't matter. Each one has a unique scent that opens the nostrils, regardless of any other powers they may or may not have. Can we agree on that point at least?

Speaking of essential oils, they're your secret weapon here. These bad boys are extracted from plants and flowers and come with a whole bunch of benefits. Lavender is my go-to, with its mind-calming vibes that can ease stress and help ya catch some Z's. Then there's ylang-ylang and chamomile, which work wonders on anxiety and tension. Warm up that oil between your hands and let the comforting warmth spread all over your palms, even before the massage begins.

Now it's time to get your hands dirty, in the best way possible. Start at the top with your head and work your way down, using your fingers and palms to knead and stroke those muscles. Pay special attention to those tight spots in your shoulders, neck, and lower back. Apply just the right amount of pressure and use gentle circular motions to release all those knots and ease the stress away. And ya gotta remember to take deep breaths, my friend. Let your body relax fully, allowing yourself to surrender to the healing touch like a sleepy kitten.

But wait, there's more to this sensory journey! Let's talk baths. Oh, the glorious sanctuary of a soothing soak. Fill up that tub with warm water and throw in some bath salts or essential oils that are known for their calming properties. Lavender is once again your best bet, along with rosemary or cedarwood. As you slip into the water, let it envelop your body and cradle you in its gentle embrace. Close your eyes and forget about the outside world for a while. This is your moment, a moment when you let the touch of the water wash away all your worries and fatigue.

And now, dear friend, we come to the power of a good ol' hug. Let's not underestimate the comfort that comes from wrapping our arms around someone we love or trust. It's like a warm, heartfelt embrace has the ability to bring solace, reminding us that we're not alone in our struggles. It's a gentle reminder that we have a support system, ready to strengthen our resilience. So go ahead, reach out to that special person in your life and let their healing touch uplift your spirit, reigniting your strength and inner peace.

Remember, my fellow mortician, self-care isn't some luxury; it's an absolute necessity. In the midst of our demanding profession, we need to make ourselves a priority. We need to honor the toll it takes on our bodies and minds. So take a moment for yourself, even if it's just for a little while. Let the healing touch be your refuge, your escape from the stress and compassion fatigue that come along with this noble line of work. Embrace it and let it remind you of the power you hold within, waiting to be nurtured and cherished.

You've got this.

Emotional Self-Care: Nurturing the Heart

The Weight of Grief

You know, being a mortician is no ordinary gig. We're the ones who take care of the departed, making sure they're ready for that one-way trip to the great beyond. It's a sacred duty, a responsibility that weighs heavy on our shoulders. But let me tell you, it ain't an easy road. The emotions that come with this job, the grief, it's like a burden we carry every day.

I can still feel that weight of grief settling on me like a thick fog. It's a constant reminder that life is fragile, and death is inevitable. Every single day, we're surrounded by sorrow. Tears flowing like rain, silence that's so heavy you could cut it with a knife, and the heart-wrenching cries that echo through the halls of our place. It's like a storm of emotions, and no one can escape its wrath, not even us.

There's this one memory that sticks with me, you know? It was on a gloomy winter morning, the kind that matches the somber mood of the mortuary. A family walked through our doors, their faces etched with unimaginable devastation. They had just lost their young daughter in a tragic accident. I saw it all happening in slow motion, as the weight of their grief settled on them like a lead blanket. As you may have guessed, when it comes to the death of a child, it hurts me more than the death of a person who has lived a full life. A child's life is so full of untapped potential, it's gut-wrenching to see one's life, and one's potential disappear in an instant.

The room fell silent, except for the occasional sniffle and muffled sob. The parents, unable to bear the sight of their lifeless child, clung to each other, crying like their hearts had been ripped out. I stood there, a silent witness to their agony, feeling the crushing weight of their sorrow seep into my own bones.

Sometimes, it's hard to draw a line between our professional duty and our own humanity. That grief becomes our own, intertwining with our own past losses and experiences. It reminds us of how fragile we all are, how fleeting life can be. It's not just a burden, but a reminder of our own mortality.

But you know what? In this sea of grief, we find purpose. We offer solace to those drowning in sorrow, showing them compassion when they need it most. We become a safe place for their pain, letting them express themselves without judgment. We can't take away their pain, but we can be there, a comforting presence in their darkest moments. And in doing so, we find solace in our own grief.

But we can't forget to take care of ourselves too. That weight of grief can drain us, lead to burnout, and compassion fatigue. We have to set boundaries, give ourselves time to recharge and seek support when we need it. Self-care is not a luxury, my friend, it's a necessity. We need to find ways to replenish our well of compassion. Hobbies, a support network of fellow morticians, therapy, whatever it takes to heal from the weight of grief.

So, my reflection on this journey is this - grief is always gonna be there, right by our side. Through personal anecdotes and heartfelt tales, I've shared the emotional impact we morticians carry. It's heavy, it seeps into our souls, but it's also a testament to the incredible purpose in what we do. Let's remember, as we navigate through the storms of grief, to take care of ourselves, to find healing in our own journey.

The Healing Power of Ritual

YOU KNOW, BEING A MORTICIAN means dealing with death and all its weight on a daily basis. It's a heavy job, no doubt about it. We're there to help families through their grief, providing guidance and support when they need it most. But let me tell you, the grief doesn't just affect them. It takes a toll on us too. We carry the stories, the pain, the loss of those we care for. It's a lot to handle and leaves us emotionally drained, vulnerable to what they call compassion fatigue.

But you know what's really interesting? In the midst of all this heaviness, there's something truly healing—the ritual. Funerals, man, they're rituals that have been around for ages. And they're not just empty traditions, let me tell you. They give structure, meaning, and a sense of closure to the ones left behind. And let me tell you something, both the grieving families and us morticians find solace and a path to healing through these rituals.

Picture this with me—this tiny chapel filled with mourners. I'm up front, running the funeral service. But I gotta tell you, it's not just about leading the way. No, it's about holding space for these grieving folks. It's about giving them the opportunity to let go of their emotions, to cry and share their grief, and to find comfort in the love and support of others.

There's this one funeral that I can't forget—a young guy, gone way too soon because of some terrible accident. The air was heavy with grief as we gathered in that chapel. But check this out, during this service, I saw the power of ritual. I saw how it transformed their grief into something beautiful, something that helped them heal. The eulogy, man, it was filled with stories and memories that brought out laughter in the midst of the tears. Lighting the candles, it brought this warm glow to the room, symbolizing eternal love and remembrance. And when we all joined in singing hymns, our voices intertwined, it was like this unity, this shared experience that I can't even put into words.

And then, when it all came to an end and I saw the families leave that chapel, there was something different about them. They had this newfound sense of peace. The ritual had given them closure, a way to say their final goodbyes and start the healing process. But you know what? It wasn't just them finding solace that day. I found it too. The collective expression of grief, being a part of that, it filled my own heart with purpose and renewal.

It's wild, but rituals have this way of touching something inside of us, digging deep into our need for connection and meaning. And in the world of morticians, where death is constantly around, we've gotta learn to embrace and honor these rituals, not just for the sake of the families we serve but for our own well-being too. By truly getting into these rituals, by being present with our own feelings and those of others, we open ourselves up to this transformative experience of healing and renewal.

But you know something? The power of rituals doesn't stop at funerals. In our day-to-day work, we come across moments of deep sorrow. And let me tell you, even in the darkest times, we can find some solace and healing through creating meaningful rituals. Something as simple as lighting a candle or saying a prayer, it can give some structure and purpose in the midst of all the grief.

I remember this one time after this devastating accident that took so many lives. The weight of that tragedy was heavy on our shoulders as we prepared for the families to see their loved ones for the last time. We knew they were shattered, their grief unimaginable. So we decided to create a ritual space in our funeral home, a place for them to gather, light candles, and share their memories.

When the families arrived, they were met with a room filled with gentle candlelight. The flickering flames danced on the walls, creating this peaceful ambiance. Each family got to choose a candle and light it in memory of their loved one. And as the room filled with warm candlelight, there was this collective healing that washed over all of us. In that sacred space, the families found solace in each other's presence, sharing stories, laughter, and tears. The ritual gave them a chance to honor their loved ones and also connect with others who understood what they were going through.

In the days that followed, I watched these families navigate their grief journey. And let me tell you, even in the midst of their pain, I saw the strength and resilience awakened by the ritual. They found a way to honor their loved ones, to keep their memories alive, and to find comfort in the company of those who understood their loss.

We, as morticians, have this amazing opportunity to guide and support those who are grieving. And by embracing and honoring the power of ritual, we can create a space for healing and renewal, not just for them but for ourselves too. Through ritual, we can turn the weight of our profession into something meaningful—a journey of emotional self-care and compassion.

Picture this: as a mortician, you embark on a journey of self-care, adopting practices that serve as soothing balm for the soul, gently easing the heaviness that comes with your unique calling.

Begin by envisioning the ritual of morning reflection. Picture yourself waking up with a sense of purpose, taking a few moments to center your thoughts. Whether through meditation, deep breathing, or quiet contemplation, this ritual becomes a gentle reminder that each new day is an opportunity for renewal and emotional fortitude.

Imagine the magic of setting daily intentions. Picture the act of consciously deciding how you want to navigate the day ahead. By articulating your intentions, you create a roadmap for emotional well-being, steering your focus toward positive and affirming perspectives.

Now, let's explore the transformative power of grounding rituals. Picture yourself connecting with the earth—whether it's a brief walk outdoors, standing barefoot on the grass, or simply taking a moment to feel the solidity beneath your feet. Grounding rituals become anchors, providing stability in the midst of emotional currents.

Envision the beauty of incorporating mindfulness breaks throughout the day. Picture short pauses where you bring your attention to the present moment. These breaks, whether a few minutes of mindful breathing or a moment of appreciating your surroundings, offer respite from the weight of the day.

Consider the magic of creating a gratitude journal. Picture yourself at the end of each day, jotting down moments of gratitude. These need not be grand; they can be small pockets of joy—a shared smile, a supportive colleague, or a comforting interaction with a grieving family. Gratitude becomes a powerful antidote to the heaviness.

Imagine the transformative power of a closing ritual at day's end. Picture a gentle winding down—a moment of reflection on the day's experiences. This ritual serves as a transition from the professional to the personal, allowing you to release the emotional weight you've carried.

Envision the beauty of creating a sacred space in your home. Picture a corner adorned with soothing elements—a candle, a plant, or meaningful artifacts. This sacred space becomes a refuge, a place to retreat and replenish your spirit.

Consider the nurturing power of engaging in hobbies or activities you love. Picture dedicating time each day to pursuits that bring you joy—whether it's reading, painting, listening to music, or any other activity that allows you to momentarily escape the weight of your responsibilities.

Imagine the magic of connecting with others who share your journey. Picture reaching out to colleagues, friends, or support groups. These connections become pillars of strength, offering understanding and camaraderie in the face of shared experiences.

Last, picture the transformative power of sleep rituals. Envision a calming routine before bedtime—whether it's gentle stretches, soothing music, or a few pages of a comforting book. These rituals prepare your mind and body for rest, ensuring you wake up rejuvenated and ready to face a new day.

In the rhythm of mortuary practice, daily rituals become a symphony of self-care. By envisioning these practices—morning reflection, setting intentions, grounding rituals, mindfulness breaks, gratitude journaling, closing rituals, creating a sacred space, engaging in hobbies, connecting with others, and sleep rituals—you forge a path to emotional resilience. Each ritual becomes a note in the melody of your life, gently lifting the heaviness and nurturing the soul of a mortician.

In the embrace of ritual, dude, we find solace. In sharing stories and shedding tears, we find healing. And in honoring the departed, we find purpose and the strength to keep going. So let's dive into these rituals, man. 'Cause in doing so, we'll find the emotional nourishment and resilience we need to navigate the challenging world of being morticians.

Finding Light in Darkness

AS A MORTICIAN, I GOTTA say, we're no strangers to diving headfirst into darkness. Every single day, we come face to face with death and witness the immense sorrow that follows. And let me tell you, it ain't no walk in the park. It can drain ya both physically and emotionally, leaving you feeling like you've hit rock bottom. It's so damn tempting to let the sadness consume you, to lose yourself in the abyss.

But hear me out, it's in these moments, when everything seems pitch black, that we've gotta actively search for the light. Trust me, I know it ain't easy. You gotta make a conscious effort to change your perspective. But when you start focusing on the little sparks of hope and joy, you'll be surprised by the solace you can find amidst the grief.

One way to bring light into the darkness is through some serious introspection. Take a minute to sit down, all by your lonesome, and really think about the impact our work has on those left behind. Sure, we might be there during people's darkest hours, but don't forget that we also have the privilege of being there for them, helping them find closure and supporting them through their grief. Every time we lend a listening ear or offer a comforting touch, we're bringing a ray of light into their lives.

I'll never forget this one time that really drove home the importance of balancing the darkness and the light. There was this young woman who had lost her husband in a car accident. Man, she was drowning in her grief, couldn't even do the simplest things. But as I guided her through the funeral planning process, I saw her start to find some comfort in all the rituals and traditions that came with death. With a little guidance and a whole lot of support, I witnessed firsthand how finding light in the darkest moments can truly transform someone's life.

Oh, and don't forget about contrasting imagery. Picture this: a candle's glow piercing through the blackest night. That shit stands out, right? Well, think of the moments of joy and beauty that coexist with the sorrow. Right in the middle of death, we get to witness life being celebrated, love being expressed, and deep connections being forged through shared grief. Those moments, even if they're gone in a flash, remind us of the absolute beauty that comes with being human.

When I look back on my years as a mortician, there's this one memory that sticks out like a sore thumb. It was a gloomy winter day, clouds blocking out any hint of sunshine. I was busy prepping the body of an elderly man while his family gathered close, sharing stories and laughter. And in that moment, despite the sorrow that hung heavy in the room, there was this undeniable sense of warmth and love. It was like the darkness itself was interrupted by a bright light. It reminded me of the strength and resilience that can be found right in the midst of grief.

Finding light in darkness ain't just about introspection and contrasting imagery, though. It's about actively building up your resilience and actively seeking out moments of joy and hope. It can be as simple as making time for self-care activities, embracing hobbies that bring you joy, or spending quality time with loved ones who lift you up. By intentionally reaching for those moments of light, you're better equipped to navigate the darkness that surrounds us.

Personally, I've found solace and rejuvenation in the small pleasures that exist beyond the walls of the mortuary. Whether it's taking a leisurely stroll in nature, getting lost in a captivating book, or indulging in a guilty pleasure hobby, these moments feed my soul and remind me that beauty still exists in this crazy world.

If I can leave you with one thing, it's this: by sharing my personal experiences and these uplifting stories, I hope to inspire my fellow morticians to actively seek out the light in the darkness. Let's build up our resilience and find joy in even the toughest moments. By embracing the duality of life and death, we can uncover beauty, hope, and light even in the darkest of times.

Honoring Our Emotional Boundaries

SO THERE I WAS, SITTING in my office after a long day at the mortuary, the weight of all those emotions weighing heavy on my shoulders. Man, let me tell you, it was one challenging day. Grieving families, heart-wrenching stories, and just a constant flood of emotions that seemed to seep into my very soul. Now, I've been in this mortuary gig for a while, so I'm no stranger to the overwhelming nature of our work. But on this day, it hit me hard, and I knew I needed to take a moment to reflect on my own emotional well-being.

You see, one of the most crucial things in this line of work is establishing and honoring emotional boundaries. It's like having a shield around you, invisible but oh so necessary. These boundaries let us empathize with the grieving families without letting their emotions take over our whole being. It's not about being cold or uncaring, no way. It's about taking care of ourselves so we can keep offering support to those who need it. I know I've talked about setting emotional boundaries before, but this is an important topic. It's what prevents us from burning out.

Let me tell you a story to show you just how important these boundaries are. A few years back, this young couple came into the mortuary to make arrangements for their stillborn baby. The pain on their faces, the tears streaming down, it was just a gut-wrenching sight. And guess what? I felt every ounce of their grief, I carried it home with me that day. I was drowning in sadness, couldn't shake it off for days. It took some serious self-reflection and self-care to get back to my normal self.

After that experience, I made sure to establish and honor my emotional boundaries. I started doing daily mindfulness practices, just taking a few minutes each morning to sit in silence, focus on my breath, and let my thoughts and emotions come and go without judgment. It helped me find a calm and centered state of mind, a place where I could approach my work with a focused and emotionally resilient mindset.

I also make a point to regularly check in with myself throughout the day, staying self-aware of how I'm doing emotionally. If I'm feeling overwhelmed, I take a short break, reach out to a colleague for support, or just take a walk outside to clear my mind. And let me tell you something, having a support network is vital. Connecting with others who understand the unique challenges of our profession, whether at networking events, support groups, or online forums, it's a game-changer. It's a safe space where we can share, seek advice, and get the support we need, reminding us that we're not alone in this crazy journey.

Now, here's the thing I've learned over the years: boundaries aren't meant to separate us from our work or the emotions of others. Nope, they're like a container for our empathy and compassion. They keep us balanced and self-aware, so we can offer genuine care while still protecting our own well-being.

So, to wrap this whole thing up, honoring our emotional boundaries is essential for us morticians. It's all about self-care and balancing our needs with providing compassionate care to those who come to us. With self-awareness, mindfulness practices, and a solid support network, we can establish and protect those boundaries. And with that, we can keep serving our community with empathy and strength.

Mental Self-Care: Nurturing the Mind

The Darkness Within: Confronting the Shadows

When I first stepped into this world as a mortician, I knew there would be challenges. But what I didn't realize was the emotional weight that would accompany this sacred work. It's like tiptoeing through the ghostly recesses of the mind, uncovering forgotten emotions that have been hiding in the darkest corners.

Every day, we come face to face with death. We see the grief etched on the faces of families, the raw pain of loss, and the fragile nature of our own existence. It leaves an indelible mark on our souls, a mark that we often neglect to acknowledge.

At first, we might think we're prepared for this journey. We couldn't be more wrong. The emotional toll of our profession catches up to us, creeping into our hearts and wearing us down. The empathy we have for others can lead to what they call compassion fatigue - a suffocating exhaustion from being continuously exposed to the pain and suffering of others.

So how do we confront these shadows that linger within us? We create a safe space, a refuge for ourselves. It starts with self-care - taking the time to look within, to reflect, and engage in activities that bring us joy and peace. It could be a walk in nature, losing ourselves in a creative outlet, or seeking therapy. These acts become our lifeline, our sustenance.

But remember, we're not alone in this dark journey. There are others who share our burdens, who have felt the weight of grief on their own shoulders. Connecting with them brings immense comfort and support. Joining support groups, seeking out mentors in our field - these avenues become our guiding light, showing us that we're not walking this path alone.

But let me tell you, the road to facing our shadows is no picnic. It demands that we confront our own mortality and come to terms with the inevitability of life's impermanence. It forces us to carry the weight of grief within ourselves and learn to release it, however painful that may be. This process can even unearth unresolved trauma from our own lives, shattering our carefully constructed walls.

Yet, we must approach this journey with compassion and patience, treating ourselves with the care we so readily give to others. We must allow ourselves the time and space to heal, to mourn, to be angry, and to expose our own vulnerability. Only through embracing these emotions can we transform our pain into strength. Only by acknowledging the darkness within can we better serve those who rely on us to guide them through their own grief.

And let's not forget about our physical and spiritual well-being. We have to take care of ourselves physically, engage in exercise, eat well, and get enough rest. Our bodies are not impervious to the toll of our work. Furthermore, nurturing our spiritual selves - through meditation, prayer, or meaningful rituals - can provide us with the inner peace and guidance we so desperately need.

But here's the thing: facing our shadows is not a one-time gig. No, my friend, it's an ongoing process. Just as grief is a journey, so too is the path of confronting our own emotional challenges. It requires a commitment to perpetual self-reflection and self-care.

By shining a light on our inner darkness, we not only find healing and strength for ourselves, but we become the compassionate guides our clients need. Our work is sacred, and by acknowledging the depths of our own emotions, we can serve others with a profound understanding that only comes from traversing the depths of our own souls.

Together, let us embrace the shadows that reside within us and emerge as morticians who are stronger, more resilient, and brimming with compassion and grace.

The Power of Solitude: Embracing Silence

THERE'S SOMETHING TRULY mesmerizing about the quiet, when words fall short and our thoughts take center stage. It's in those moments of solitude and stillness that I've uncovered something extraordinary, an unparalleled force that heals and restores our weary minds. Trust me, I've come to appreciate the profound impact of silence on our mental well-being.

Personally, I've found solace in nature, a magical place where I can escape the weight of the world and bask in the beauty surrounding me. One day, as the burden of work grew heavier, I sought refuge in a nearby forest. Walking through the towering trees, I could feel my worries melting away, replaced by an overwhelming sense of peace. A babbling brook guided me to a quiet spot, where I immersed myself in the tranquility of the moment. It was there, as I communed with the Earth, that I realized despite the pain I witnessed daily, beauty and resilience still thrived. Nature became my sanctuary, a place where my burdens lifted and my spirit found renewed strength.

But nature is not the only avenue to embrace the beauty of silence. Meditation became my lifeline, providing a respite from the constant onslaught of emotions that come with my profession. In the face of unbearable grief, when the weight of my shoulders threatened to crush me, I turned to meditation. Creating a haven in my home, surrounded by candles and incense, I dedicated precious moments each day to silence. I closed my eyes, focusing on my breath, allowing my thoughts to drift by like wisps of clouds. And with each inhale and exhale, a burden lifted, replaced by a calm, a tranquility that silenced the chaos within. In those moments of blessed silence, I rediscovered control over my thoughts and emotions, finding the strength I needed to carry on.

You see, the toll of being a mortician cannot be underestimated. Our profession is one of compassion and service, but it also reminds us of our own fragility. That's why embracing solitude and the beauty of silence is vital to our well-being. For me, journaling has been an incredibly effective way to find solace in the midst of solitude. With pen in hand, I pour out my heart onto the blank pages of a journal, releasing the emotions that threaten to overwhelm me. Each evening, as I sip on steaming tea, I lose myself in the act of writing. The pen glides with ease, untangling the knots in my mind and offering a space to heal and reflect. In journaling, I've found a safe haven, a place to unload the burdens I carry, creating room for healing and self-discovery.

In a world that values noise and busyness, solitude and silence often go unappreciated. But for morticians, they're essential. They allow us to reconnect with ourselves, find solace away from the chaos of our profession. By immersing ourselves in solitude through nature, meditation, or journaling, we can nurture our souls, replenish our spirits. Prioritizing self-care, embracing silence becomes a reminder that we too deserve moments of stillness and rejuvenation.

So, in my journey as a mortician, I've come to understand the transformative power of solitude and silence. In those moments of stillness, our minds find solace, our spirits are replenished. Whether it's immersing ourselves in nature's embrace, delving into the depths of meditation, or letting our thoughts take flight on the pages of a journal, we must embrace silence. It's the key to reconnecting with ourselves, finding inner peace amidst the chaos of our work. Amidst the pain and grief, morticians must foster self-care and embrace the transformative power of solitude. And in that embrace, we'll find the strength and renewal to continue our important and compassionate work.

From Grief to Gratitude: Cultivating Emotional Resilience

LISTEN UP, MORTICIANS, let's not treat grief like it's the plague. I get it, we all run for the hills when we feel it creeping in. But you know what? We need to embrace it. Yeah, I said it. Grief is like that stubborn guest you can't kick out of your house. It's there for a reason, and trust me, once you let it in, healing starts to happen.

Here's a little trick I've learned: grab a journal and start pouring your soul onto those pages. No judgment, just raw emotions and thoughts. It's like a therapy session with yourself. This bit of self-reflection can be a game-changer, helping you process your grief and better understand all those complicated feelings. And guess what? It'll make you one hell of an empathetic support system for others.

Grief has a sneaky way of messing with our heads. It twists our reality and forces us to question everything, even our own mortality. But here's the kicker: it's also an opportunity to grow and become a freaking superhero. Yeah, you heard me right.

One thing I want you to try is practicing gratitude. I know, sounds absurd when you're knee-deep in sadness, right? But trust me, it works. Start acknowledging all the tiny blessings in your life, and watch the magic happen. Suddenly, healing becomes possible. And get this, embracing mindfulness practices is a game-changer too. It keeps you present with your emotions, accepting yourself with love and compassion. You're like a peaceful island amidst a stormy sea. Those thoughts and feelings? They're just passing waves, not knocking you down.

Let me level with you: grief ain't no linear path with some dot at the end. It's an unpredictable rollercoaster ride that slaps you with life lessons left and right. But guess what? These lessons are pure gold. They help us build emotional muscle and appreciate the hell out of life.

One vital lesson is the fragility of life. It reminds us that every damn moment counts. It's about living with purpose and making self-care a priority. We gotta take care of ourselves, nurture our emotions, and check-in. Another lesson? We need each other. In our profession, we got a tight-knit community, people who know the struggles and joys we face. Connect with them, find solace, and build a support system that carries you through the darkest times.

In the realm of mortuary practice, where the heart often carries the weight of profound emotions, envision the transformative journey of cultivating emotional resilience. Picture this: as a mortician, you stand not only as a guardian of the departed but as a steward of your own emotional well-being. Embrace the empowering rhythm of building resilience—nurturing the ability to weather the storms and emerge stronger, like a resilient tree swaying gracefully in the face of the wind.

Begin by picturing the essence of self-awareness. Imagine tuning into your own emotions, recognizing their ebb and flow. Self-awareness becomes the compass guiding your journey, helping you navigate the sometimes tumultuous waters of your profession with a deep understanding of your own emotional landscape.

Now, let's explore the magic of reframing challenges. Picture the ability to view difficulties not as insurmountable obstacles but as opportunities for growth. By shifting your perspective, challenges become stepping stones, each one contributing to the construction of your emotional resilience.

Envision the transformative power of a support network. Picture yourself surrounded by colleagues, friends, and loved ones who understand the unique challenges of your profession. This network becomes a safety net, a collection of compassionate hearts ready to offer understanding and encouragement when the weight feels particularly heavy.

Imagine the beauty of setting boundaries. Picture the strength that comes from recognizing your own limits and having the courage to establish clear boundaries. By creating a protective space around your emotional well-being, you cultivate resilience that allows you to bounce back from challenging moments.

Envision the transformative dance of adaptability. Picture yourself adjusting to the ever-changing cadence of your work. Like a skilled dancer adjusting to different tempos, your ability to adapt becomes a source of strength, ensuring you remain agile in the face of unpredictability.

Consider the nurturing power of mindfulness. Picture moments of being fully present, engaging with each experience without judgment. Mindfulness becomes a calming rhythm, allowing you to approach challenges with a clear and centered mind, fostering emotional resilience.

Imagine the transformative power of self-compassion. Picture treating yourself with the same kindness and understanding you extend to others. Self-compassion becomes a soothing melody, offering solace in moments of self-doubt and fostering a sense of inner strength.

Envision the beauty of finding joy in small moments. Picture yourself celebrating the simple pleasures that bring you happiness—a shared smile, a comforting conversation, or a moment of connection. Joy becomes a resilient thread woven into the fabric of your everyday life.

Now, picture the transformative journey of learning from experiences. Imagine viewing setbacks not as failures but as lessons. Each experience, whether positive or challenging, becomes a valuable note in the symphony of your growth, contributing to your emotional resilience.

Last, envision the beauty of embracing a positive mindset. Picture the power of focusing on what you can control, cultivating optimism, and acknowledging the silver linings in difficult situations. A positive mindset becomes a beacon of light, guiding you through the darker moments with unwavering resilience.

In the heartbeat of mortuary practice, emotional resilience becomes the rhythm that sustains you. By envisioning these practices—self-awareness, reframing challenges, a support network, setting boundaries, adaptability, mindfulness, self-compassion, finding joy, learning from experiences, and embracing a positive mindset—you foster a resilient spirit. It's a journey of strength, where each beat of emotional resilience propels you forward, enabling you to face the demands of your profession with grace and fortitude.

So, here we are, at the end of this wild ride. The path from grief to gratitude ain't no joke, but guess what? You're ready to take it head-on. Embrace those emotions, reframe your perspective, and find strength and compassion deep within your soul. You're not just navigating your profession, my friend, you're uncovering the secret superpower of grief. Strap in, follow the tips and exercises I've shared, and embark on this journey with an open heart and fierce determination. Let's navigate together, morticians, and conquer the path from grief to gratitude.

Unveiling Vulnerability: Embracing Authenticity

YOU KNOW, IN OUR LINE of work, we come face to face with some intense emotions from others. We see the pain and heartache that comes with losing someone, and it can be tempting to shut ourselves off and stay detached as a way to protect ourselves. But when we do that, it's like we're denying ourselves the chance to really connect with the people we're supposed to be helping. It's through vulnerability that we can build those real connections and provide caring and understanding.

Thinking back on my own experiences, there was a time when I struggled with this whole idea of vulnerability. I always prided myself on being professional and keeping it together when tragedy struck. But there was one moment that stands out, a moment that shattered that wall I had built. I met a grieving spouse who just radiated pain, and I couldn't help but be overwhelmed with emotion myself.

In that split second, I had a choice to make. I could keep up the act of being a stoic professional, or I could let my guard down and honestly show how I felt. I chose the latter. I cried alongside that spouse, offered a tight hug, and truly let myself be there in their moment of sorrow.

What happened was incredible. By embracing my own vulnerability, I not only brought comfort to the grieving spouse, but I also grew as a person. I learned the importance of shared humanity. Our vulnerabilities are what connect us all. It's through our weaknesses and struggles that we experience the full range of human emotions and form deep connections with others.

Imagine this: as a mortician, you navigate the delicate dance between professionalism and authenticity, realizing that the beauty of your work lies in the genuine connections you forge. Embrace the empowering rhythm of authenticity—letting your true essence shine through like a radiant light in the somber corridors of your profession.

Begin by picturing the essence of self-discovery. Imagine the process of exploring and understanding your values, beliefs, and passions. Authenticity blooms when you have a deep awareness of who you are and what truly matters to you.

Now, let's explore the magic of vulnerability. Picture yourself embracing the courage to be vulnerable, allowing others to see your authentic self. Vulnerability becomes the bridge that connects you with colleagues, families, and the departed, fostering genuine connections based on openness and honesty.

Envision the transformative power of self-expression. Picture yourself communicating authentically, letting your unique voice resonate in your interactions. Whether it's in the way you speak, the words you choose, or the empathy you convey, your authentic expression becomes a source of strength and connection.

Imagine the beauty of accepting imperfections. Picture the freedom that comes with embracing your flaws and quirks.

Authenticity isn't about perfection; it's about being real, unapologetically imperfect, and embracing the beauty in your uniqueness.

Envision the transformative dance of aligning actions with values. Picture yourself living in accordance with your deeply held beliefs. Authenticity shines when your actions reflect the principles that guide your life, creating a harmonious dance between your values and your daily practices.

Consider the nurturing power of embracing feedback. Picture yourself open to receiving constructive criticism and feedback. Authenticity grows when you approach growth with humility, acknowledging that there's always room for improvement and learning.

Imagine the transformative power of genuine connections. Picture the joy that comes from forging connections based on authenticity. Whether with grieving families, colleagues, or within your personal life, authentic connections become the heartbeat of meaningful relationships.

Envision the beauty of celebrating diversity. Picture yourself appreciating and embracing the diverse perspectives and experiences that surround you. Authenticity flourishes in an environment where differences are celebrated and respected.

Now, picture the transformative journey of staying true to yourself in challenging moments. Imagine navigating difficult situations with authenticity, responding in a way that aligns with your values rather than succumbing to external pressures. Authenticity becomes a guiding compass in times of adversity.

Last, envision the beauty of self-compassion. Picture yourself treating your authentic self with kindness and understanding. Authenticity isn't about perfection—it's about being gentle with yourself, acknowledging your humanity, and fostering a compassionate relationship with the person you are becoming.

In the heartbeat of mortuary practice, authenticity becomes the rhythm that resonates through your work and interactions. By envisioning these practices—self-discovery, vulnerability, self-expression, accepting imperfections, aligning actions with values, embracing feedback, genuine connections, celebrating diversity, staying true in challenging moments, and practicing self-compassion—you infuse your profession with the genuine essence of who you are. It's a transformative journey where authenticity becomes a guiding force, enriching your work and relationships with depth, sincerity, and an unmistakable authenticity.

To help you on your own journey of self-discovery, I dive into the power of storytelling and reflective exercises. Through storytelling, I encourage you to explore your vulnerabilities and the experiences that have shaped you. By sharing these stories, we can break down the barriers that keep us apart and create a space of understanding and connection.

One exercise that I find incredibly powerful is creating a "Vulnerability Inventory." It's all about reflecting on times when we've felt vulnerable in the past and understanding the lessons we learned from those moments. By uncovering these vulnerabilities, we can start seeing them as strengths rather than weaknesses.

For instance, I share a personal story about losing a close friend. In the midst of my grief, I found solace in opening up to others and sharing my pain. It was through that vulnerability that I discovered the power of human connection and how comforting it can be to let others support us in tough times.

Alongside storytelling and self-reflection, I also stress the importance of self-care practices that encourage vulnerability and authenticity. This might involve things like journaling, mindfulness exercises, or therapy sessions that help us get in touch with our emotions. These practices help us become more self-aware and gain a deeper understanding of our own vulnerabilities.

Ultimately, my hope is that you understand that embracing vulnerability isn't a sign of weakness, but rather an act of courage and self-acceptance. When we drop the facade and show our true selves, it invites others to do the same. And that creates a safe space for genuine connections, both in our personal lives and in our roles as morticians.

As we go on this journey of self-discovery, I genuinely hope you come to realize that vulnerability is not something to avoid or be afraid of. It's actually a fundamental part of being human. It's through our vulnerabilities that we truly connect with others, offer empathetic care, and find meaning and fulfillment in our lives as morticians. So let's reveal our vulnerability and embrace our authentic selves, because it's through that real connection that we can truly thrive.

The Healing Power of Creativity: Expressing the Unspoken

WHEN I FIRST STARTED out as a mortician, man, I had no idea what I was getting myself into. I thought it was just gonna be about prepping bodies and getting them ready for their final resting place. But it's so much more than that, my friends. It's about seeing how fragile life really is, witnessing the tragedy of loss, and feeling the weight of grief that families carry on their shoulders. It takes a whole lot of emotional strength, compassion, and empathy to do this job. I mean, if we don't find healthy ways to cope with all the death and grieving, it'll mess us up big time.

You know what I've discovered though? Creativity, man. It's like this superpower that helps us express ourselves and heal at the same time. It's like channeling all those heavy emotions into something tangible and meaningful. When we're creative, we can give voice to the unsaid, and it's this beautiful thing, man.

A lot of us morticians find solace in writing. Whether it's keeping a journal, writing poems, or even working on a novel, it gives us a space to make sense of all the crazy emotions we go through. I've found so much comfort in writing about my experiences, using it as a sort of therapy to reflect on the lives I've come across and how they've impacted me. When I put pen to paper, I feel like the weight of it all gets lifted, and suddenly, everything becomes a little clearer.

And then there's painting and other visual arts, man. They offer a whole different way of expressing ourselves. With colors and textures and all that, we can show emotions that words just can't capture. In my studio, I've painted so many scenes from funeral services, capturing all those intense moments of grief and remembrance. As I get lost in the brushstrokes, I can feel all those pent-up emotions being released. It's like bringing the unspoken into the light, you know?

And we can't forget about music, my friends. Music is like a magic potion for the soul. Whether we're playing an instrument or just jamming out to a song that hits us right in the feels, music has this incredible power. I've had so many moments sitting at my piano, my fingers dancing across the keys, feeling like I've opened up a doorway between what we see and what we can't put into words. Music reaches the deepest parts of us, helps us process emotions that are too intense for words alone.

As morticians, we have this unique privilege, man. We get a front-row seat to all the raw emotions that come with death. We see people in the depths of grief, stunned by shock, and navigating all the little nuances of remembering their loved ones. And while we're navigating all that, it's crucial that we take care of ourselves, too.

Getting into creative stuff, man, it's not just about expressing ourselves. It's also about finding new ways of looking at things, gaining insights, and discovering all those hidden depths within ourselves. When we engage in artistic pursuits, we tap into the wellspring of our own emotions and connect with others who get it, you know?

There's this poet dude named Rumi, and he said, "The wound is the place where the Light enters you." And I think, man, that through the healing power of creativity, we let that light in. It shines a path to healing, a path that's deeply personal and introspective, but man, it's necessary.

So, my fellow morticians, I want to invite you to embrace your creative side. Whether it's writing, painting, playing music, or whatever else gets your creative juices flowing, give yourself permission to express all the stuff that words can't capture. Dive deep into those emotions that we encounter daily and let creativity be the thing that helps you transform, man.

In the next chapters, I'm gonna dive into specific creative practices that can help us on our self-care journey as morticians. I'm talking writing prompts, painting exercises, and even music recommendations that touch the soul. We'll explore all these cool ways of tapping into our creative wellspring.

Just remember, my friends, that even though our work deals with darkness, our souls have the power to find light through creative expression. Let's go on this journey together, embracing the transformative nature of art, and find some solace, release, and strength in the beautiful creative processes that make each of us unique.

Finding Support: Connecting With Peers and Mentors

The Power of Connection

Man, being a mortician can really take a toll on you. I mean, we're constantly surrounded by loss, grief, and pain. It's like we're stuck in this world of intense emotions and death, dealing with these heavy matters day in and day out. It can be isolating, you know? But here's the thing, we're not alone in this. We've got each other, and that connection? It's a lifeline that helps us handle the stress and compassion fatigue while also allowing us to grow as individuals and professionals.

When I first got into this gig, I was hit with this overwhelming sense of responsibility. The long hours, the constant exposure to death, and the toll it took on me emotionally? It was wearing me down. There was this one stretch that was particularly brutal. I remember sitting in my office late at night, feeling completely drained. I was weighed down by the events of the day, and this sadness had settled deep within me. I couldn't escape it. Just staring at the mountain of paperwork on my desk made it even worse. And then, my phone buzzed, interrupting the dark cloud hanging over me. It was a message from Sarah, a fellow mortician I know.

"Hey, I can tell you've had a tough one. Want to grab a coffee and talk?" Her message read.

I can't even describe how much that simple act of reaching out meant to me. It was like she was throwing me a lifeline. I quickly replied, feeling a glimmer of hope ignite deep within me. We decided to meet up at this cozy little café nearby, and before I knew it, I was pouring my heart out to Sarah.

We sat there, with the steam from our cups of coffee swirling around us, and Sarah listened like her life depended on it. I spilled my guts about all the emotions and difficulties that were eating me alive. And you know what? She got it. She understood the weight of this job, the toll it takes on your mental and emotional well-being. In that moment, I realized I wasn't alone in this struggle. Sarah's empathy and understanding made me feel seen, heard, and validated in a way I had never experienced before.

As the evening came to an end, Sarah dropped a piece of advice on me that stuck with me ever since. She stressed the importance of building connections within the profession. Those connections would be our lifeline, she said. Something to rely on when things got tough, when we were stressed out, or when we just needed someone to share the burden with. I had this epiphany right then and there about how impactful these connections with our peers and mentors could be for our well-being.

From that day forward, I started actively seeking out other people in the field. I went to conferences, joined online communities, and reached out to experienced morticians who could be mentors. And you know what? Those connections became my support system. We formed this tight-knit community that understood the unique challenges we faced on a daily basis.

Over time, those connections turned into genuine friendships. We leaned on each other during the tough moments and celebrated the victories together. Late-night phone calls became the norm, filled with words of encouragement and shared experiences. We'd meet up for spur-of-the-moment coffee dates, where we could let our guard down and just be ourselves without any fear of judgment.

Through those connections, I finally found that sense of belonging I had been searching for. It was like finding my tribe, you know? These were people who spoke the same language and understood all the unsaid struggles that came with our chosen profession. We cheered each other on, we laughed together, and we were there to catch each other when one of us stumbled.

But you know what? The power of connection went beyond just finding a sense of belonging. These relationships also brought fresh perspectives and new ideas to the table, enriching my work as a mortician. We shared experiences and knowledge, pushing me to grow not only personally but professionally too. I explored new techniques and approaches to my work because of what I learned from these connections.

In moments when the emotional burden got too heavy, my connections within the profession reminded me of why I do what I do. They reminded me of the impact we have on the lives of those we serve, and the honor it is to be entrusted with such a delicate task. Most importantly, they reminded me that this journey isn't one I have to navigate alone. There are others out there who know exactly what it's like to feel all those emotions.

So, to my fellow morticians out there who are feeling the weight of this profession on their shoulders, reach out. Connect. Build that network of support. Find those mentors who can guide you and peers who can lift you up. Embrace the power of connection because let me tell you, it's through these relationships that we find understanding, support, and the strength to keep doing this important work. Together, we can conquer the challenging waters of this profession and come out the other side stronger, more resilient, and even more compassionate.

Finding Your Tribe

AS SOON AS I DIPPED my toes into the world of being a mortician, I felt completely adrift, drowning in the waves of emotions that came crashing down on me. The weight of grieving families, the endless hours spent elbows deep in the embalming room, and the constant presence of death – it all started to tear away at my mental and emotional state. It was in the midst of this chaos that I finally understood the immense value of finding my tribe.

I kicked things off by diving headfirst into industry events, desperate to build up a crew of kindred spirits. These gatherings turned out to be a treasure trove of wisdom and experience. Seasoned morticians spilled their guts, sharing tips, tricks, and tales of both triumph and catastrophe. And in the process, a camaraderie like no other started to bloom. Suddenly, I was surrounded by people who got it, who understood me on a level I had never thought possible. These events also gave me the chance to stay up-to-date with all the latest trends and innovations, soaking up knowledge from the absolute best in the business.

But it didn't end there. I knew I needed more, so I joined professional organizations, seeking not only networking opportunities but also a sense of belonging. These groups planned regular meet-ups, seminars, and conferences that were the perfect melting pot for like-minded morticians. We all faced the same challenges, shared the same love for our craft, and straight-up got each other. The bond we formed during those interactions was indescribable. We swapped advice, dished out empathy, and held each other up tight, united by our shared mission: giving the dearly departed and their families the most compassionate care we could muster.

And let's not forget about the marvels of social media, my friends. It's never been easier to connect with fellow morticians from every corner of the globe. Facebook, Instagram, LinkedIn – pick your poison, and you'll find a thriving community of death enthusiasts. Online forums and groups have become my sanctuary, a place where I can let loose, talk about my experiences, ask for advice, and offer support to others. Through these platforms, I've gotten to know folks from all walks of life, gaining a broader perspective on our extraordinary line of work. And let me tell you, it's a reminder that we are all woven into a much larger tapestry than we might realize.

When it comes to finding your tribe, you've got to be picky. Seek out the ones who share your values, interests, and ambitions. Find those who truly understand the importance of taking care of yourself mentally and emotionally. Being able to open up about the heartaches and triumphs of our profession with those who genuinely understand the emotional baggage we carry is a godsend. Their shared experiences, their wisdom, their guidance – it's a lifesaver, pulling us through those dark times and lifting us up when joy comes knocking.

Belonging to a community that truly gets the challenges and rewards of our line of work opens up a world of possibilities. It's not just about emotional support and a shoulder to lean on – it's about personal growth and professional development too. There's something magical about being connected to battle-worn souls who have seen it all. Their expertise, their insights, their finger on the pulse of the industry – it's priceless.

Oh, and let's not forget about the burnout. It's a very real threat in our line of work. But by surrounding ourselves with others who have faced the same demons, we can learn coping mechanisms, self-care strategies, and resilience-building techniques. Our tribe breathes new life into us, reminding us that we are not alone in this demanding, emotionally draining profession.

To wrap it all up, let me just say this: finding your tribe within the mortuary profession is absolutely essential. Dive headfirst into networking events, join professional organizations, and make connections through social media. Build a kick-ass community that understands you, supports you, and empowers you. These people will be your rock on this wild journey of self-care, offering a safe space for growth, knowledge, and emotional well-being. Together, we will navigate the complexities of our line of work, taking solace in the simple fact that we are never alone.

Nurturing Mentorship

MENTORSHIP, MAN, IT'S like the backbone of the mortuary profession. It hooks up the newbies with the seasoned vets, passing on knowledge and insights that you won't find in some textbook. Throughout history, mentorship has been the real deal when it comes to developing those mortician skills and keeping the principles of our profession alive. My parents were great mentors, but I feel that to be more well-rounded, I would need to seek out other morticians of all skill and experience levels.

When I think back to the early days of my career, I can't help but think of the mentors who shaped me into who I am today. There was this dude named William, an old-school mortician with more experience than I could even imagine. I'll never forget our first sit-down. He just sat there, listening to me ramble on about my dreams, and then he dropped some serious wisdom. He told me to get a solid education, but he also stressed the importance of empathy and compassion. It's not just about burying bodies, man. It's about being there for people during their toughest times.

Under William's wing, I started to see mentorship as the key to personal and professional growth. He had my back from the get-go, teaching me all the technical stuff like embalming and funeral planning. But he also made sure I took care of myself, reminding me that this job can really mess with your head if you're not careful.

I can't even begin to describe how much I've changed because of William's mentorship. With his guidance, I learned how to handle those gut-wrenching situations, have those tough talks with grieving families, and most importantly, take care of myself. He was always there to challenge me, celebrate my wins, and make me think about the way I was doing things.

Finding a mentor who's on your level, who understands what you're going through, bro, it's essential. But let me tell you, it ain't always easy. Sometimes you gotta put yourself out there, connect with the people you admire in the industry. Go to conferences, workshops, networking events - the whole shebang. That's where you'll meet the experienced folks who can give you some real knowledge.

But here's the thing, my dude, you gotta establish that trust, that bond with your mentor. It can't just be some shallow connection. You gotta show a genuine interest in their work, actually care about what they have to say. And trust me, they'll see that and be more likely to give you the time of day.

Once you find that mentor, you gotta be open to feedback. They're gonna give you some criticisms, and it's on you to take it like a champ. Don't get all defensive and think they're trying to tear you down. They just want to see you succeed, man.

And when you've learned all that good stuff and become the seasoned vet yourself, don't forget to pay it forward. Be a mentor to some newbies, pass on that knowledge and wisdom. It's all about keeping this profession alive and kicking, you know?

I've been lucky enough to be on both sides of the mentorship game, and let me tell you, it's made all the difference. From Sarah, who had my back during some tough times, to Michael, who blossomed into a kick-ass pro under my guidance, that mentorship thing is something else.

It's not just about us individuals, man. Mentorship creates this ripple effect that goes beyond our growth. It preserves our wisdom, keeps our practices ethical and compassionate. And it brings us together, creating that sense of community and brotherhood that makes this job worth it.

So to sum it all up, mentorship is the key to success in this profession. The guidance and wisdom from the OGs can set you on the right path, help you navigate the craziness. But it ain't gonna fall into your lap, my friend. You gotta actively seek it out, build those connections, and never stop learning. Mentorship, it's a journey, and it's a damn good one.

The Role of Peer Support

BEING A MORTICIAN, let me tell you, it's quite the gig. It's noble and essential, sure, but it sure does come with its fair share of challenges. I mean, dealing with death day in and day out really takes a toll on our emotions. We end up feeling drained and isolated too often. But you know what? We're not alone in this crazy profession. We've got our fellow morticians, our comrades in this macabre world, who understand us and have our backs.

When I first jumped into this line of work, I had no clue just how heavy the emotional burden would be. The never-ending hours, the constant exposure to grief, and the pressure to be the strong one for the devastated families can crush our spirits. But let me tell you about this one time when I hit rock bottom and reached out to a seasoned mortician named Sarah. We met up for a cup of coffee, and as we started swapping stories, I could almost feel the weight being lifted off my shoulders.

Sarah, bless her soul, she knew the struggle. She had been in the game for years, seen it all. She shared her tales of dealing with compassion fatigue and how she managed to stay sane all these years. Her words gave me comfort, let me know that what I was feeling was totally normal. She reminded me that it was okay to take care of myself and that seeking support wasn't a sign of weakness, but a sign of strength.

But getting support from our peers is about more than just getting validation and a shoulder to lean on. These folks have lived through experiences that have shaped them, and by listening to their stories, we gain wisdom and learn new ways to cope with the heavy load we carry. It's like we're building our very own toolbox of resilience.

I still remember this one support group meeting I went to. Talk about eye-opening. Each of my colleagues had their own unique ways of looking out for themselves. Some found solace in nature, soaking up the peace of the outdoors. Others turned to art to express themselves. It was through these conversations that I discovered my own avenues of self-care that resonated with my soul.

But one of the most powerful things about peer support is the chance to vent. Let's face it, our line of work can stew up a whirlwind of emotions, and sometimes we just need someone who gets it to let it all out to. Having a fellow mortician who knows the ins and outs of our profession makes the whole venting process not only a way to release pent-up emotions but a way to feel empowered as well.

During one particularly rough patch, I reached out to my buddy Mark. We met up in a local park, away from the funeral home, and let it all pour out. In that vulnerable moment, I realized just how heavy the weight I was carrying alone had become. Just letting it all out was so transformative. It reminded me that I wasn't alone in this journey, that there were others who knew exactly how it felt, and that together, we could conquer anything.

But our comrades in the mortician realm don't just listen and nod their heads; they also offer words of encouragement and motivation when times get tough. They've been there, done that, got the t-shirt, and can be our guiding light through the darkest of times.

One instance always sticks in my mind. I had just gone through a week that was emotionally draining like no other, and I was feeling the weight of it all. I confided in my colleague Emma, who had this amazing ability to lift others up. She reminded me of the purpose behind what we do, how we help families find closure. Her words hit me deep, reigniting my passion and reminding me of the positive impact we can have on others' lives.

Peer support, my friends, is an absolute must for the well-being of us morticians. It's not just about validation and comfort; it's about perspective, insight, and encouragement too. By sharing our stories, letting out our frustrations, and exchanging advice, we create a lifeline in a profession that can be isolating and exhausting. With our comrades by our side, we can tackle the unique challenges we face and keep our minds sharp and happy.

Navigating Online Communities

LET ME TELL YOU, IN today's crazy interconnected world, the internet is like gold when it comes to networking and professional development. And don't think the mortuary profession is exempt from jumping on this digital bandwagon. Oh no! We morticians have jumped right in and found our own little haven in the form of online communities. Trust me, these places are a lifesaver for all of us who deal with dead bodies day in and day out. They offer support, camaraderie, and a sense of not being alone in this weird and wonderful profession.

One of the greatest things about these online communities is finding people who are just as nuts about mortuary stuff as you are. I mean, whether you're a newbie mortician who needs some guidance or a seasoned pro who loves sharing their knowledge, online forums and social media groups are the place to be. Seriously, you'll meet all sorts of folks in these communities - funeral directors, embalmers, grief counselors, cremation specialists - you name it. And let me tell you, having a network of colleagues who really get what you're going through is priceless.

But wait, there's more! These online communities also provide a space for continuous learning. I'm talking about discussions on everything under the sun related to the mortuary profession. From embalming techniques to grief counseling methods, you can dive deep into any topic you fancy. And the best part? You'll hear from professionals with diverse backgrounds and expertise, which means you'll get insights you never even thought of before. It's like having a virtual classroom right at your fingertips.

And here's the cherry on top: resource sharing. Oh man, the members of these online communities are always posting articles, industry updates, and must-read books. It's like having your own personal news feed tailor-made for your mortuary passion. Staying up-to-date with the latest trends and developments in the field has never been easier. And let me tell you, that knowledge doesn't just help you professionally - it also allows you to provide better care for your clients and support for grieving families. Talk about a win-win.

Now, with the ocean of online communities out there, you need to know how to navigate these bad boys effectively. Here are my top tips:

First, choose the right platforms. Look for ones that match your interests and needs. You want to join communities that are active, well-moderated, and filled with professionals who share your values. Make sure to join both general mortuary forums and specialized groups that focus on your specific interests within the field.

Second, engage like a boss. When you participate in discussions, be a thoughtful contributor. Be respectful and considerate of other people's perspectives, even if they don't align with yours. Share your own experiences and insights, but don't forget to listen and learn from others too. This is a give-and-take situation, my friend.

Third, here's where the online world really shines - anonymity. Take advantage of the fact that you can be real and honest without anyone knowing who you are. Share your struggles, seek advice, and open up about your vulnerabilities. These communities are a safe space where you won't be judged or misunderstood. So, go ahead and spill your guts.

Next, avoid burnout. Consider this your friendly reminder to set boundaries and manage your time wisely. It's easy to get sucked into these communities and lose track of reality. But remember, self-care is vital, so don't let it fall by the wayside.

Lastly, embrace diversity. These online communities bring together professionals from all walks of life. Don't shy away from engaging with people who have different perspectives and experiences than yours. You'll be amazed at how much you can grow and learn when you challenge your own assumptions. So, be open-minded, my friend.

In the end, online communities are a lifeline for us morticians. They give us support, connection, and a chance to grow professionally. So, don't miss out. Join these digital havens, find your people, engage in awesome discussions, and take advantage of the wealth of knowledge and resources available. But remember to navigate these communities like a champ: choose the right platforms, engage thoughtfully, embrace your anonymity, avoid burnout, and open your mind to diverse perspectives. You got this!

Overcoming Stigma and Judgment

BEING A MORTICIAN IS no easy task. Our job is to honor the departed and provide comfort to grieving families, but society doesn't always see it that way. We're often facing judgment and stigma because of outdated beliefs and misrepresentations in movies and TV shows. It's tough to feel proud of our work when people have these misconceptions.

When I was young, I was approached with a sort of curiosity and stigma for being associated with morticians for parents. Sometimes people would be nice to me, I thought they were my friend, until they would ask to see, "where the work happens." And I realized they were just being friendly because they wanted to see dead people. Other times, when I had actual friends and potential boyfriends, their parents would ask what my parents did, you know, in that horrible way that people do to gauge how much respect they think you deserve, and well, what was once a cheery face, always turned dour and angry. As though my mentioning of that profession reminded them of everyone they had ever known who passed away and me and my parents were to blame. I rarely heard from a friend again after that.

I'll never forget the first time I encountered judgment after becoming a mortician. I was at a party, surrounded by acquaintances, and someone asked me what I did for a living. As soon as I mentioned I was a mortician, everything went quiet. The room seemed to freeze, and I could feel the discomfort hanging in the air. It was like I had become an outsider in my own social circle. Some people even started whispering, their voices heavy with curiosity and judgment.

But I've come to realize that these reactions don't define me or the importance of my role. They're just a reflection of people's discomfort with death and the funeral industry. It's easier for them to stick to stereotypes instead of facing the reality of mortality. They'd rather stay in their bubble of preconceived notions than engage in a real conversation.

To overcome all the stigma and judgment, we need to have confidence in ourselves. We have to remember that our work matters, that it has deep meaning, and deserves respect. That confidence can come from embracing our passion for this profession, acknowledging the positive impact we make on people's lives, and recognizing the unique skills and expertise we bring to the table.

Setting professional boundaries is another crucial part of overcoming stigma and judgment. When faced with disrespectful remarks or invasive questions, we have the right to set limits. We don't have to engage in conversations that undermine our worth or perpetuate stereotypes. By politely redirecting the conversation or choosing to disengage from discussions that don't serve our well-being, we're asserting our dignity and professionalism.

Teaching others about our profession is another powerful tool in combating stigma and judgment. People often fear what they don't understand. By busting myths and providing accurate information, we can challenge the assumptions and stereotypes that contribute to negative perceptions. It can be as simple as having open conversations, sharing our personal experiences, or participating in community outreach programs. By educating others, we pave the way for a more compassionate and informed society that recognizes and respects the significance of our work.

Promoting understanding is closely tied to education. By humanizing our profession, we generate empathy and combat the fear that fuels judgment. Sharing stories of the individuals we've cared for, the families we've supported, and the impact our work has on the community can shift people's perspectives. When they see us as compassionate professionals dedicated to providing comfort during life's toughest moments, their judgment transforms into admiration, appreciation, and acceptance.

The stigma and judgment we face as morticians can be disheartening and challenging. But by cultivating self-confidence, setting professional boundaries, educating others, and promoting understanding, we can rise above these obstacles and embrace our role with pride and resilience. We're the ones who uphold dignity and respect, guiding families through their darkest times. It's about time society recognizes and honors the profound importance of our work.

Seeking Professional Help: When to Reach Out

Recognizing the Darkness Within

Let me tell you, my path to this realization wasn't a smooth ride. It was like a roller coaster of sheer horror that left an imprint deep in my mind. I'm talking faces etched with grief, bodies so still they might as well be statues, and the stench of death that lingered in the air. It became a twisted kind of normal for me, being a mortician and all. But let me tell you, the impact of those scenes started to mess with my head. It was like the weight of the whole damn world was sitting on my shoulders, slowly chipping away at my resilience like a freaking jackhammer.

I used to rely on sleep to escape from the horrors of the day, you know? But now, sleep was a distant memory. Restlessness became my best friend at night, while the faces of the dead haunted my dreams. Those lifeless eyes stared right through me, blaming me for their fate. It was like they thought I had some kind of control over life and death. And let me tell you, I questioned the fragility of life, the whole mortality thing, and the unbearable pain that seemed to seep into every moment of my life.

It wasn't just the death scenes that messed with me, though. It was the emotional toll. Constant exposure to grieving families took its toll on my heart. Their pain became my pain, and I was drowning in sorrow like a sinking ship. I couldn't even separate their grief from my own anymore. The lines blurred and I lost myself in the process.

My once sparkly and optimistic spirit disappeared, leaving behind a void that nothing could fill. Even the simplest tasks felt like climbing Mount Everest. It was like the weight of the world was in my bones, just crushing me bit by bit. I wondered how much more I could handle before I crumbled completely.

But here's the kicker, okay? This darkness forced me to confront the fear of asking for help. Society had drilled it into me that asking for help was a sign of weakness. I mean, come on! As a mortician, I was supposed to be this strong, unbreakable pillar. But as I teetered on the edge of my own unraveling, I realized that reaching out for help wasn't a flaw. It was a brave freaking move toward healing.

It took guts for me to step out from behind the curtain, to admit that I couldn't do it alone. I sought out the guidance of a therapist who helped me navigate the maze of my own mind and emotions. Together, we dove deep into the trauma and grief that had taken hold of me for way too long, pulling apart those knots that kept me trapped. Therapy taught me how crucial self-care is, how I needed to find moments of peace in the chaos. I discovered the power of managing my mind and staying present. And man, having a support system of friends and loved ones who got it was a game-changer.

But above all, I learned to be freaking kind to myself, to acknowledge my limits and cut myself some slack.

As the darkness lifted, I found myself again. My resilience came back in full force, and that weight on my shoulders became a badge of honor rather than a burden. Yeah, the journey sucked big-time, but it was necessary. Facing my struggles head-on was the only way to find my way back to healing and self-care.

And you know what? I'm sharing my story because I want other morticians in the same boat to know that they're not alone. There's always a flicker of light in the darkest corners. Seeking help doesn't make us weak, it makes us badass. Self-care isn't just a luxury, it's a freakin' lifeline in our line of work. And as we start this self-care journey, we gotta remember to treat ourselves with the same love and empathy that we give to others.

The Breaking Point

BEING A MORTICIAN WAS always something I took pride in. I mean, day in and day out, I was surrounded by death and grief, providing comfort to families who were going through unspeakable pain. But, you know what? I soon realized that while I was there for everyone else, I had neglected to be there for myself. It's like all those years of witnessing sorrow and loss had slowly chipped away at my own well-being, and before I knew it, I was drowning in a sea of emotions I had buried deep down.

So, it was just a regular Wednesday evening when everything came crashing down. I had just finished embalming a body and was finalizing the funeral arrangements in the back office. The silence of the room was eerie, with only the slight hum of the air conditioner filling the air. It was like the atmosphere was mirroring the weight that I had been carrying. And let me tell you, that weight felt heavier than a ton of bricks.

Out of nowhere, this wave of sadness hit me like a tidal wave. It was as if I had been sucker-punched right in the gut. The tears welled up in my eyes and before I knew it, they were pouring down my face, hot and furious. All those pent-up emotions that I had tried to hide were now gushing out, overwhelming me completely. I reached out for something, anything, to hold onto, but all I felt was this sense of being lost in the midst of it all.

I sank into my chair, my body shaking with the force of my tears. It was a release, I'll give it that, but it was also terrifying to realize just how fragile I had become. I mean, for so long, I had put on this brave face, thinking that I was invincible. But in that moment, I had no choice but to confront the harsh reality that I was just a regular human being, capable of breaking like anyone else.

As I sat there, drowning in sadness, I knew I couldn't keep carrying this burden alone. The isolation had only made it worse, like an invisible vice grip on my heart. I had hit my limit, and it was crystal clear that I needed help.

Then, it hit me. I remembered a conversation I had months ago with my good friend, Sarah. She had mentioned this therapist who specialized in trauma and compassion fatigue. At the time, I brushed it off, thinking I didn't need any help. But now, in the depths of my despair, her words echoed in my mind like a lifeline.

With trembling hands, I picked up my phone and dialed the number she had given me. The voice on the other end was soothing and understanding, assuring me that they could assist. I scheduled an appointment for the next day, and for the first time in a long time, I felt a glimmer of hope creeping back into my life. It was my first step towards reclaiming my own well-being and finding the strength to continue doing what I loved.

So, there I was, sitting in that therapist's office the next day, unraveling the layers of pain I had carried for far too long. I poured my heart out, sharing the sorrows I had witnessed, the grief I had internalized. And you know what? That therapist listened. I mean, really listened. They offered validation and guidance on how to navigate the unique challenges of my profession.

In that sacred space, I began my healing journey. Yeah, it wasn't easy. Opening up and being vulnerable was scary as hell, but it was necessary. Through therapy, I learned coping strategies to set boundaries, to take care of myself, and to reach out for support. It was a journey towards self-compassion and resilience, and man, did I need that.

Looking back, that breaking point was one of the best things that could have happened to me. It forced me to face the reality that I couldn't carry the weight of the world on my own. It pushed me to ask for help, to tear down the walls I had built around myself, and to find comfort in the support of others.

Today, I'm still a mortician, still facing the challenges of my job. But you know what's different? I approach it all with a newfound understanding of the importance of self-care. I prioritize my well-being just as much as I prioritize the well-being of the families I serve. And when that weight of grief threatens to consume me, I reach out for help without hesitation, knowing that I'm not alone in this journey.

So, as I share my story with you, my fellow morticians, I want you to know that it's okay to break. It's okay to crumble under the weight of your own humanity. Because in those vulnerable moments, we learn the true strength of the human spirit and the power of seeking support. We can't be effective caretakers of others if we neglect to take care of ourselves.

The Road to Recovery

SO, LET ME TELL YOU about the first step I took on my road to recovery – therapy. I was desperate for some help, someone who could understand all the trauma and grief that goes hand in hand with being a mortician. And let me tell you, finding a therapist who specialized in that was like finding a needle in a haystack. But I got lucky. Really lucky. This therapist knew exactly what I was going through and the toll it takes on our mental health.

Now, these therapy sessions were no walk in the park. Nope, they were more like tearing open old wounds and reliving moments of heartache and loss. It hurt like hell, I won't lie. But man, did it set me free. Through therapy, I began to understand how my trauma had seeped into every corner of my life. And most importantly, I learned how to finally acknowledge and validate my own damn emotions. Something I had been neglecting for far too long.

But therapy wasn't enough for me. I needed more. So, I went searching for support groups – a place where I could vent and share my struggles with people who actually got it. And boy, did I hit the jackpot. These groups were filled with other morticians who knew exactly what I was feeling. I mean, these guys had stress and compassion fatigue flowing through their veins too. Being amongst them, hearing their stories, and offering my own support and encouragement... It was like finding my tribe. And suddenly, I didn't feel so alone anymore.

On top of therapy and support groups, I took time for myself – self-care, baby! I found joy in painting, gardening, and yoga. These activities gave me an escape from the constant demands of my job and allowed me to reconnect with the person I used to be before all this mess. And if that wasn't enough, I also made damn sure I took care of my physical health. Eating healthy, exercising, and getting enough beauty sleep – that stuff mattered too, you know? Turns out, taking care of my body was just as important as taking care of my mind.

Oh, and believe me, I had to learn the hard way about setting boundaries. In my line of work, it's so easy to get sucked into everyone else's problems that you forget about your own. Well, not anymore. I learned to say no, to delegate, and to make my own self-care a priority without feeling guilty. And let me tell you, that was a tough pill to swallow. But it was necessary. I had to put myself first, for once.

All these tools and resources, man. They transformed me – inside and out. I built up my resilience, my hope, and my sense of control. I can honestly say that I no longer feel like I'm drowning in the weight of my profession. No way. I feel strong, empowered even. And I'm eternally grateful that I embarked on this journey to reclaim my mental and emotional well-being.

And speaking of that journey, let me put it out there – it ain't no straight line. Nah, it's more like a rollercoaster ride. Filled with ups and downs, setbacks and breakthroughs. It's a wild ride, for sure. But man, is it worth it. Through therapy, support groups, self-care, and the bravery to ask for professional help, I've regained control of my own damn well-being. It's a story of resilience, hope, and the transformative power of putting yourself first. And I hope, more than anything, that my journey can inspire other morticians who are dealing with their own stress and compassion fatigue. Because let me tell you, healing is possible – even in the face of the toughest challenges. So, let's take care of ourselves, man. Take care and keep helping others with the compassion and professionalism we know best.

Breaking the Stigma

AS A MORTICIAN, I'VE been through the wringer when it comes to dealing with the stigma attached to this line of work. Back when I first stepped into the funeral home, I was filled with excitement about being able to bring some solace and closure to grieving families. But let me tell you, as I dove headfirst into the job, that emotional toll hit me like a freight train. The endless hours, the never-ending line of mournful faces, and the gut-wrenching stories all started to wear me down. And when I reached out to my colleagues for support, well, let's just say reality slapped me across the face. They brushed off my concerns, telling me to toughen up and reminding me that this was par for the course. The unspoken message was clear: as morticians, we need to be tough and unflinching in the face of death and grief.

People love us when they need us. When they don't need us, they don't like to be reminded we exist.

But why the heck do we have to shoulder this burden alone? Why can't we be allowed to acknowledge and deal with our emotions without having judgment and stigma come crashing down upon us? These questions haunted me day and night, pushing me to dig deeper and uncover the truth. So, I started talking to my fellow morticians - past and present - and guess what? Turns out, we're all carrying the same heavy load. Many of them have felt that same pressure to keep their emotions locked away and pretend like they're invincible.

I spoke to this retired mortician, who, for reasons she preferred to keep to herself, went by an alias. She poured her heart out to me about being on the verge of burnout for years without seeking help. She wore the weight of her job like a shackle, terrified that admitting she needed a lifeline would be a death sentence for her career. It wasn't until she retired that she realized just how much damage this stigma had done to her mental health. Just like so many of us, she cared tirelessly for others while neglecting herself in the process.

But let me tell you, the stigma doesn't stop at just us morticians. Society as a whole has got some mighty twisted misconceptions about what we do, and that only adds fuel to the fire when we need help. People have this notion that we're immune to crumbling under the weight of it all just because we're around death all day, every day. It's like they think we're some kind of emotionless robots. Well, let me tell you something. We're just as human as everyone else, and we feel the weight of grief and loss every single day. Don't you dare for a second belittle the incredible emotional labor we put into this job.

Here's the real deal: no matter how tough we might seem, we're not made of stone. Compassion fatigue, vicarious trauma, and burnout are demons we battle just like any other helping profession out there. Our hearts break with every loss we witness, and our minds are constantly wrestling with the enormity of grief. It's high time we face up to these emotions and find healthy ways to handle them.

If we're going to stomp out this stigma, we need to start by creating a community that's all about compassion and support. Let's rally around self-care and encourage open dialogues about mental health. Instead of shrugging off our own struggles or brushing off the toll this job takes on us, let's make spaces where morticians can openly ask for help without fear of being shamed. We've got to set the record straight about what our profession truly entails and educate society about the emotional weight we carry. By doing this, we'll not only uplift our fellow morticians, but we'll also lay the foundation for future generations entering our field.

Don't get me wrong, breaking this stigma won't be easy. It's going to take us leading by example and putting our own mental health front and center. Seeking professional help when we need it should be seen as an act of strength, not weakness. We've got to realize that we can't pour from an empty cup, and only by taking care of ourselves can we continue to provide the compassionate support grieving families need. So, let's band together, shatter the silence, and build a community where self-care is valued above all else. It's time to prioritize our mental health and make it the heartbeat of our profession.

Faith and Resilience: Finding Meaning in Your Work

The Dark Night of the Soul

I can't tell you how many nights I've spent tossing and turning, haunted by the faces of the people we've laid to rest. The grief-stricken families, the tears streaming down their faces, the heart-wrenching sobs that echo in my mind—it's enough to make you feel completely helpless and lost. In those moments, it's so easy to lose sight of what the hell we're even doing here, to doubt the impact we're making, and to wonder if it's all worth it.

But let me tell you something: finding faith and resilience in the face of all that despair is crucial. It's what gets you through those dark nights of the soul and brings you back to the path of purpose and meaning. Faith can come in all shapes and sizes—maybe it's a belief in a higher power, or in the interconnectedness of all things, or maybe it's just believing in the power of human compassion. Whatever the hell it is, that faith is what leads us out of the darkness.

But here's the thing, finding that faith ain't no easy task. It's a journey that requires you to dig deep within yourself, to confront all your fears and doubts head-on. And let me tell you, that darkness can be downright overwhelming. It feels like it's gonna swallow you whole. But it's in that darkness that you find your true strength, your resilience. It's in facing your doubts and fears that you discover just how damn compassionate and empathetic you can be.

For me, one way to hold onto that faith and resilience is through self-care. Taking the time to nurture yourself physically, emotionally, and spiritually is absolutely crucial. It can be as simple as taking a walk in nature, practicing some damn mindfulness or meditation, or just doing things that bring you joy and peace. Prioritizing self-care creates a space within yourself where that faith and resilience can grow.

And let's not forget the importance of leaning on your fellow morticians. Connecting with those who understand the unique challenges we face can be a lifeline in times of despair. Sharing our stories and experiences gives us strength and encouragement, letting us know that we're not alone in this struggle. And you know what? We can learn a whole lot from each other too, picking up new perspectives and strategies for dealing with the emotional toll of what we do.

Listen up, my fellow morticians who might be going through your own dark nights of the soul, I've got something to say. Have faith in yourself and in the work that you're doing. Even in the darkest moments, you're making a goddamn difference. Take care of yourself and reach out for support from those who get it. Embrace the darkness as a chance for growth and self-discovery. And remember, the light will always come back, guiding you back to that path of purpose and meaning.

A Beacon of Light

I'VE ALWAYS BELIEVED in the power of faith and spirituality. It's something that was ingrained in me by my parents since I was a child. They taught me that there's something beyond our understanding, a force that gives us the strength to face any challenge that comes our way. And let me tell you, that belief has been an anchor in my journey as a mortician, guiding me through the turbulent waters of grief.

There was one particular case early on in my career that truly solidified my belief in the power of faith. It was the funeral of a young child, a life that was tragically cut short. The heaviness in the room was so palpable that when I approached the grieving parents, I could feel sadness wash over me like a wave crashing on the shore.

In that moment, I realized that my role as a mortician went beyond the practicalities of preparing a body for burial. I was there to offer comfort and support, to be a ray of hope in the darkness of grief. So, I reached out to the parents, offering my deepest condolences and a listening ear. In their time of despair, I understood just how vital faith is.

Religion and spirituality have always played a central role in the mortuary profession. Throughout history, from ancient funeral rituals to the customs we practice today, the belief in an afterlife and the power of prayer have provided solace to those who are left behind. It is through faith that we find meaning in the face of death, hope that there's something more to this existence, peace for our departed loved ones, and trust in a higher plan.

For us morticians, faith and spirituality are not just abstract concepts, they're a source of strength and guidance. They give us a framework to understand and navigate grief, allowing us to connect with the families we serve on a deeper level. Whether it's through religious practices, meditation, or simply taking a moment to reflect, nurturing our spiritual selves is crucial for our own well-being.

I've witnessed firsthand how faith and spirituality can transform the lives of those who have experienced profound loss. I once met a widower who had lost his wife of fifty years. Whenever we spoke, he would talk about finding solace in attending religious services and praying for his wife's soul. His faith gave him a sense of peace and comfort that helped him navigate the complexities of grief while honoring his wife's memory.

Now, I'm not saying faith is a cure-all for the pain and sorrow we encounter. But it can be a guiding light when darkness threatens to overwhelm us. It reminds us to hold onto hope, to find comfort in the fact that there's something bigger at play in the universe. In moments of despair, it's our faith that helps us carve a path forward, to continue providing care and support to those who place their trust in us.

In conclusion, faith and spirituality are essential for the well-being of morticians. They give us the strength to face grief head-on, the wisdom to find meaning in our work, and the compassion to support those who mourn. By nurturing our faith, we can better navigate the challenges in our profession and fulfill our duty to walk alongside the bereaved. When darkness threatens to consume us, it's our faith that becomes a beacon of light, guiding us on our path and illuminating the lives we touch.

Finding Meaning in the Mundane

YOU KNOW, FINDING MEANING in our work isn't always easy. It's like we're stuck in this cycle of just going through the motions, seeing our tasks as nothing more than obligations. But what if we shifted our perspective? What if we started looking at our work as a chance to honor the lives of those who have passed?

When we embalm a body, we're not just preserving flesh and bones. We're preserving memories, legacies, and stories. We're keeping alive the essence of who that person was. It's about more than just the physical - it's about the soul.

And let's not forget about faith. So many of us in this profession find comfort in our religious or spiritual beliefs. It's like we draw strength from a higher power, using our faith to guide us through the challenges we face. Our work becomes more than just a job - it becomes a sacred calling to bring comfort to the grieving, honor the deceased, and uphold the dignity of every life we encounter.

But it's not just about what we do in the embalming room or at the funeral service. It's about the everyday moments, the small acts of kindness that can make a lasting impact. It's in the compassionate conversations we have with grieving families, the gentle touch as we dress and prepare the deceased, and the attention to detail in every aspect of our work. It's about showing up and being there for people when they need it most.

And let's not forget to be present. Mindfulness is key. When we fully engage in each task, whether it's arranging flowers or comforting someone who's lost a loved one, we can find purpose and fulfillment in the ordinary. We're able to connect with the living while still honoring the memory of the deceased.

But you know what else? We need to take care of ourselves too. It's so important to prioritize our own well-being. We can't pour from an empty cup, as they say. Rest, reflection, and rejuvenation are essential. Taking time for self-care allows us to show up with compassion and empathy day after day. Whether it's meditation, journaling, or doing something we love, like a hobby, we need to nourish our hearts and minds.

Finding meaning in our work is a personal journey. It takes self-reflection, intention, and an open heart. But when we embrace the impact we have on others, seek connection with our faith, and engage mindfully in our work, something extraordinary happens. We transform the routine into something truly meaningful.

As morticians, we have the privilege of serving others during their most vulnerable moments. By finding meaning in what may seem mundane, we can truly make a difference. So let's embrace the power we have and create something extraordinary out of the ordinary.

Navigating the Valley of Tears

LET ME TELL YOU ABOUT Sarah's story. You see, Sarah was always the go-to person for her friends when they were in a bind. She had this ability to lend an ear and provide comfort like no other. It was no wonder that she ended up in the mortuary profession, a place where she could offer support and care to those suffering from unimaginable loss.

But let me tell you, Sarah quickly realized that her chosen path wasn't a walk in the park. The weight of grief that she carried on her shoulders every single day was suffocating. Each body she prepared, each family she comforted, left an imprint on her soul that she just couldn't shake off.

Sarah's journey through the valley of tears was rough, let me tell you. It was like she was drowning in sorrow, constantly weighed down by the collective grief of all those families she encountered. But you know what kept her going? Faith. Prayers became her lifeline, a way to stay connected to something bigger and find the strength to push through the pain.

Through her faith, Sarah gained a new perspective. She realized that being a mortician wasn't just about providing a service, it was about being a vessel for healing and comfort. It was a sacred duty that demanded compassion and empathy. So, the valley of tears became sacred ground for her, a place where she could offer solace to those who needed it most.

But let me tell you, navigating that valley wasn't easy. Sarah had to learn some practical strategies to cope. Emotional boundaries and self-care became crucial. She figured out that she couldn't help others if she neglected herself, so she made it a priority to take care of her own emotional well-being.

Sarah also learned the value of seeking support from others who understood her profession. She joined a support group for morticians where she could share her experiences and find comfort in the company of those who truly understood the toll their work took on their hearts. It was a lifeline for Sarah, a reminder that she wasn't alone in her struggles.

Finding healing amidst the pain was an ongoing process for Sarah. She knew she couldn't just brush off the burdens she carried, but with time and self-compassion, she learned to embrace the tears and let them flow. Crying wasn't a sign of weakness for her, it was a testament to the depth of her empathy and love for those she served.

In her journey through the valley of tears, nature became Sarah's refuge. She would take walks in the woods, relishing in the quiet solitude and finding solace in the rustle of leaves and the ancient presence of trees. Nature became her sanctuary, a place where she could pour out her grief and find renewal.

You know what Sarah realized through all of this? Navigating the valley of tears required strength, resilience, and a whole lot of compassion. It changed her, transformed her into a person who understood the depths of pain and had the ability to guide others through their darkest hours. Despite all the tears and struggles, she made a difference in the lives of others.

Sarah's story showcases the emotional toll of the mortuary profession and the resilience it takes to navigate that valley of tears. It serves as a reminder that amidst the sorrow and grief, there is still room for healing and transformation. By embracing the tears and finding strength in faith and community, morticians can guide others through their darkest hours while also finding solace and renewal for themselves.

The Gift of Presence

WHEN I FIRST STEPPED into the world of being a mortician, I had this idea in my head that all I needed to do was carry out the necessary tasks to prepare the deceased for their final resting place. It was a job, just a job. But guess what? Life has a funny way of throwing curveballs at you. And it wasn't until I met those grieving families who were desperately in need of a compassionate car and a shoulder to lean on that I realized there was so much more to this gig than meets the eye.

One family, in particular, comes to mind. They were huddled together in the small chapel of our funeral home, faces etched with grief. They had just lost their mother, a woman who radiated vibrancy and was the heart and soul of their family. To say that their pain was tangible would be a huge understatement. Standing there with them, I could feel their sorrow seeping into my own bones, creating an ache that mirrored their own.

In that moment, something shifted within me. The realization hit me like a ton of bricks: my job wasn't just about embalming bodies or arranging funeral services. No, my purpose extended way beyond that. It was my duty to be present for these families, to create a safe space for their grief, and to offer them solace during their darkest hours. I couldn't change what had happened, but I could be there for them, to show support and let them know they weren't alone in this bewildering journey of loss.

Through years of experience and deep personal reflections, I've come to understand just how crucial our presence is in someone's grieving process. It goes beyond words and actions; it's about the energy we bring, the space we hold, and the acceptance we offer. Being fully present means being emotionally available, truly listening, and demonstrating empathy without judgment.

To be present is to clear our minds of our own needs, concerns, and distractions, and truly focus on the person right in front of us. It demands our full engagement, requires us to shelve our own grief and stress, and prioritize the healing journey of those we're here to serve. Now, I won't lie to you, it's not always a walk in the park. Sometimes, when we've faced our own losses or compassion fatigue threatens to collapse our spirits, being present can seem like an uphill battle. But hey, here's the kicker: the gift of presence is something that we need to nurture and cultivate, like a delicate flower in a garden.

One way I've found to enhance our capacity to be present is through faith. Many of us in this line of work draw strength from our spirituality and belief in something bigger than ourselves. Turning to our faith can anchor us in our purpose and give us the resilience we need to hold space for others. It reminds us that life is sacred, even in the face of death, and helps us find meaning and hope amidst the tears.

In my personal journey, I've discovered that incorporating rituals and prayers into my daily routine has worked wonders. Whether it's a moment of silence before diving into the day's work or a prayer asking for strength and guidance, these practices connect me to a force greater than myself and help me approach each interaction with grace and compassion.

Moreover, seeking support from fellow morticians or joining a faith-based community can provide the much-needed sense of belonging and understanding that sustains us in this role. Knowing that we're not alone in our struggles offers opportunities for growth and learning, and boy, don't we all need that in this line of work?

But here's the thing, my friend, faith is a personal journey. What works for one may not click for another, and that's absolutely fine. The key here is to explore different spiritual practices and find what brings you comfort and peace within the turmoil.

Being present with those who are grieving isn't about having all the answers or waving a magic wand to make their pain disappear. It's about creating a space where they can freely express their emotions, share their cherished memories, and be heard without judgment. It's about respecting the privilege of being invited into their raw vulnerability and holding their grief with utmost tenderness and compassion.

In all my years as a mortician, one thing has become crystal clear to me: the gift of presence is a two-way street. Yes, while we offer our support and comfort to those who are grieving, we also receive so much in return. We bear witness to the resilience of the human spirit and the power of love. We are humbled by the reminder of our own mortality and the urgency of cherishing every single moment. And above all, we are entrusted with an immense responsibility during one of life's most challenging chapters.

So, as we navigate the intricacies and complexities of this role, let's never forget the transformative power of being fully present. Let's approach each interaction with the kind of compassion and empathy that leaves no room for doubt. And most of all, let's remember that our presence itself is a gift—one that has the ability to bring light into the darkest of moments and provide solace in the face of immeasurable loss.

In the end, it's not just a job we're doing. It's a calling. A calling to be there for others in their darkest hours. A calling to be a beacon of light and hope amidst the storm. And that, my friend, is something worth holding onto.

In today's fast-paced world, where distractions abound and demands seem never-ending, the art of being present has become increasingly elusive. Yet, amidst the chaos of modern life, cultivating presence offers a pathway to deeper connection, inner peace, and profound fulfillment. In this essay, we will explore the significance of presence and offer practical strategies to embrace it in our daily lives.

Presence, at its core, is the state of being fully engaged and aware in the present moment, free from the constraints of past regrets or future anxieties. It is the ability to immerse ourselves completely in whatever we are doing, whether it's savoring a meal, engaging in conversation, or simply breathing in the beauty of nature. While it may seem simple in theory, true presence requires practice and intentionality.

One of the first steps towards cultivating presence is developing mindfulness—the practice of non-judgmental awareness of the present moment. Mindfulness encourages us to observe our thoughts, emotions, and sensations with curiosity and acceptance, rather than getting swept away by them. Through mindfulness meditation, we can train our minds to focus on the present, anchoring ourselves in the here and now.

Another essential aspect of presence is learning to let go of distractions and embrace simplicity. In today's digital age, we are bombarded with constant stimuli, from emails and social media notifications to the pressures of multitasking. By decluttering our physical and mental spaces, we create room for stillness and presence to flourish. This might involve setting boundaries with technology, creating sacred rituals for reflection, or simply taking moments of solitude to reconnect with ourselves.

Furthermore, fostering presence requires us to cultivate a deeper awareness of our surroundings and the people around us. Too often, we move through life on autopilot, oblivious to the beauty and richness of our environment. By practicing gratitude and paying attention to the small details, we can awaken to the wonders that surround us each day. Additionally, investing in meaningful connections with others—listening attentively, offering genuine empathy, and sharing moments of vulnerability—deepens our sense of presence and belonging.

Moreover, integrating mindfulness into our daily activities can help us infuse presence into every aspect of our lives. Whether it's mindful eating, mindful walking, or mindful communication, these practices invite us to slow down, savor the moment, and engage with a sense of openness and curiosity. By approaching each experience with a beginner's mind, we cultivate a sense of wonder and awe, transforming even the most mundane tasks into opportunities for growth and connection.

Cultivating presence is not a destination but a journey—an ongoing commitment to showing up fully and authentically in every moment. By embracing mindfulness, simplifying our lives, nurturing meaningful connections, and infusing mindfulness into our daily activities, we can awaken to the richness of life and experience a profound sense of joy and fulfillment. As we embark on this journey of presence, let us remember the words of Thich Nhat Hanh: "The present moment is filled with joy and happiness. If you are attentive, you will see it."

Renewing Your Purpose: Finding Meaning in Service

A Ray of Light in the Darkness

Man, let me tell you about this one Monday morning at the mortuary. It was one of those gloomy days where you feel like the whole weight of the world is on your shoulders, ya know? As soon as I walked in, this strong smell of embalming fluids hit me, mixing with the fresh scent of flowers on the tables. Behind the scenes, we morticians knew that this job demanded much more than just professionalism.

The dang phone kept ringing off the hook, and each call brought news of another life lost. Body bags were metaphorically piling up, man, a constant reminder that we ain't invincible. We just went about our tasks, doing everything mechanically and sticking to the routine. But sometimes, even that routine fails us.

That day, we got a call about this young woman who had taken her own life. Preparing her body for viewing, it hit me like a ton of bricks. The room felt so heavy, bro, like you could hear our hearts breaking through the silence. Her life was gone, just like that, leaving behind this gaping emptiness that was hard to put into words.

As I stood there, looking at her lifeless form, I couldn't help but wonder what could have brought her to this point. Was it a cry for help that nobody heard? Or did she genuinely believe that death was her only escape? Those questions stayed with me, man, haunting me like a ghost. I felt guilty, like I had somehow let her down by not being able to stop this tragedy.

The days that followed were a blur of funeral arrangements, grieving families, and private tears shed when no one was watching. The collective grief was suffocating, man, threatening to swallow us whole. We morticians had become experts at stuffing our emotions in a box, putting on a brave face for others while we battled our own demons.

But then, something incredible happened. We got a letter, addressed to the funeral home. Opening it up, I felt tears welling up in my eyes as I read the heartfelt words inside.

"Dear Sir or Madam," the letter began. "I had to take a moment to thank you for the care and compassion you showed when my sister passed away. Your professionalism and kindness made all the difference in our grieving process. We were lost and broken, but you helped us find a way through the darkness."

That letter went on, man, describing how the small acts of comfort we offered meant the world to that family. A warm cup of tea, a listening ear—it was those little things that gave them solace when they needed it most. It was a reminder that even in the midst of grief and pain, we had the power to make a difference, to bring some light to their lives.

From that moment on, I made a promise to myself. I swore to never let the heaviness of this job overshadow those moments of light that shone through. Yeah, we were gonna keep experiencing heartbreak and exhaustion, but we also had the chance to bring comfort, solace, and closure to these grieving families.

Throughout the years, I kept that letter close to my heart. It became my guiding light during those darkest days, reminding me that our work as morticians wasn't in vain. It was a beacon of hope, showing me just how much we could impact the lives of others.

As I look back on that tough day and the letter that came afterwards, it reminds me of the delicate balance we morticians have to strike. We gotta find that sweet spot between sorrow and joy, between grief and solace. That's where we find our own self-care, man, recharging our compassion and resilience so we can keep serving others in their most vulnerable moments. And in that tightrope act, we find our own little ray of light in the pitch-black darkness.

Embracing Vulnerability

THROUGHOUT MY CAREER, there have been countless moments where I've found myself in the presence of grieving families, their pain and sorrow radiating through the room. These moments, I must admit, were quite intimidating at first. But as I took the leap and allowed myself to be vulnerable, something incredible happened. The walls came down, and a newfound connection and trust formed.

One particular instance stands out vividly in my memory. I was at a funeral home, surrounded by a sea of tear-streaked faces and engulfed by a heavy silence. The weight of their grief settled onto my shoulders, and I couldn't help but feel empathy welling up inside me.

In that moment, I did something brave. I chose to let my guard down and share my own experiences of loss, expressing my sincere sorrow for their unimaginable pain. And you know what? I let the tears fall alongside the mourning family, defying the societal expectation for morticians to remain stoic. Though it shocked them at first, my act of vulnerability became a bridge, connecting us on a profound level. They appreciated my willingness to open up and truly share their pain, and it created a space for them to express their emotions more freely.

But vulnerability doesn't just deepen the bond with grieving families; it also brings mortuary colleagues closer together. We're often surrounded by high-pressure environments that can overwhelm us with the emotional weight of our responsibilities. It's tempting to put up walls and isolate ourselves to cope, but there's something special that happens when we let vulnerability in.

I remember a particularly challenging period at the funeral home. We had dealt with an unexpectedly high number of tragic deaths in a short span of time, and it almost broke our spirits. Instead of retreating further into our own sadness and frustration, we decided to gather for a meeting where we each shared our vulnerabilities and struggles. It was a chance for us to let go of our masks and lean on one another for support.

Sharing our vulnerabilities not only brought us closer as a team, but it also allowed us to brainstorm coping strategies and offer practical support. We organized self-care workshops and implemented a buddy system for regular emotional check-ins. In our shared vulnerability, we discovered strength we didn't know existed. It reminded us that we weren't alone in our struggles and that together, we could conquer even the toughest challenges.

Of course, embracing vulnerability isn't without its fears and resistance. We morticians are conditioned to maintain professionalism and distance. The fear of judgment or rejection often holds us back from fully embracing our vulnerability. We worry that showing our emotions might make us appear weak or incapable in the eyes of our colleagues or the families we serve. And what if our emotions cloud our judgment or ability to navigate difficult situations?

These fears are absolutely valid, but they shouldn't stop us from experiencing the profound opportunities that vulnerability can bring. Embracing vulnerability doesn't mean throwing professionalism out the window. It means recognizing that we're human beings with emotions and that connecting on a deeper level can bring comfort and solace to those experiencing immense grief.

To truly embrace vulnerability, we must start with self-reflection. Take the time to identify the fears and resistance holding you back. What societal expectations or beliefs are keeping you from embracing vulnerability? Write them down and challenge their validity. Understand that vulnerability isn't weakness; it showcases our capacity for empathy, compassion, and genuine connection.

Once you've acknowledged your fears, start small by taking calculated risks. When appropriate, share a personal experience or emotion with a grieving family. Let yourself be present in their sadness and show them that their loss affects you too. By demonstrating vulnerability, you create an environment that encourages honest communication and builds trust between you and the families you serve.

And it's not just about embracing vulnerability with families. It's equally important to foster an environment of vulnerability within your professional circle. Encourage open dialogue and create opportunities for colleagues to share their experiences, fears, and challenges. By forming a support network of understanding individuals who know the unique pressures of our profession, we can navigate the emotional complexities of mortuary work together.

Lastly, remember that vulnerability is a never-ending journey. It requires consistent self-reflection, courage, and the willingness to step outside your comfort zone. It won't always be easy, but the rewards are immeasurable. Deeper connections with grieving families, a sense of purpose and fulfillment in your work, and a support system that can carry you through the toughest of times.

By allowing yourself to be vulnerable, you open doors to deeper connections and trust with grieving families and colleagues alike. Through self-reflection, overcoming fears, and taking calculated risks, you embark on a journey of self-discovery and purpose in your work. Remember, vulnerability isn't weakness; it's a strength that enhances your professional interactions and brings profound meaning to your role as a mortician.

Caring for the Caregiver: Supporting Your Team

Creating a Culture of Support

Being a mortician is no easy task, let me tell you. Every day, we find ourselves knee-deep in a world that demands our utmost attention. Death becomes a constant companion, lurking in the shadows and leaving us feeling drained, overwhelmed, and downright exhausted. But hey, that's why having a supportive team is crucial. And believe me, it makes all the difference in the world.

When it comes to building a culture of support, the first thing you gotta do is open up those lines of communication. I mean, how else are you gonna know what's going on with your team? Encourage 'em to speak up, share their thoughts and ideas. Whether it's through team meetings or one-on-one conversations, let them know their voice matters. Trust me, it'll create an environment where everyone feels heard and respected.

Now, listening may not seem like a big deal, but let me tell you, it's the glue that holds everything together. When someone on your team approaches you with their worries or challenges, listen up! Put away your distractions, look 'em in the eye, and show genuine interest. Don't just brush it off, really try to understand where they're coming from. It goes a long way in building trust and letting 'em know you've got their back.

Empathy, my friend, is a superpower. It's all about stepping into someone else's shoes and feeling their emotions. When you practice empathy, you're better equipped to connect with your team members and provide the support they need. Acknowledge their struggles, validate their feelings, and give 'em a boost of encouragement. Let 'em know they're not alone, that you genuinely care.

But hey, support ain't just an individual thing. It's about working together, playing as a team, you know what I mean? Encourage your team members to support one another, to have each other's backs. Get 'em involved in team-building activities or group projects. Basically, create an atmosphere of camaraderie. Not only will it strengthen the ties within your team, but it'll also boost productivity and job satisfaction.

Oh, and let's not forget about professional growth. Look, investing in your team's development shows 'em you value their skills and believe in their success. Think workshops, training programs, or even resources for self-learning. It'll not only enhance their abilities but also boost their confidence and overall job satisfaction.

Now, here's a biggie: recognizing and appreciating your team's efforts. Don't just let 'em toil in the shadows, give 'em their moment in the spotlight. Celebrate their successes, provide regular feedback, and for the love of all that is good, just say thank you. By recognizing their hard work, you're not only lifting their spirits, but you're also showing 'em their worth, that they're an integral part of the team.

Creating a culture of support isn't a one-and-done deal, my friend. It's a continuous journey that requires effort and commitment. So, make sure you're regularly reviewing your strategies, figuring out what works and what doesn't. And don't forget to ask your team for their input, 'cause guess what? They're in this with you. Trust me, this journey may be long, but the impact it'll have on your team's well-being and overall success will be well worth it.

In the end, building a culture of support is essential for us morticians. It helps us cope with the emotional toll our profession takes on us. By nurturing open communication, active listening, and empathy, we create an environment where our team members feel valued, respected, and supported. And let me tell ya, when we have strong relationships with our colleagues, our work just gets better. Throw in a dash of professional development, recognition, and teamwork, and you've got a recipe for success. So, remember, my friend, the journey towards support never ends, but it's a journey that'll make all the difference in the world.

Recognizing and Addressing Burnout

YOU KNOW, BEING A MORTICIAN is no easy gig. We're constantly faced with the heavy emotions that come with this line of work. We see families torn apart by grief, we have to handle some truly traumatic situations, and all the while, we're expected to maintain a level of professionalism that can sometimes feel impossible. It's no wonder that burnout sneaks up on us, affecting us mentally, emotionally, and physically without us even realizing it.

So, how do we combat this burnout? Well, the first step is recognizing the signs. While they can vary from person to person, there are some common indicators that we need to be aware of. Emotional exhaustion is a big one. It's like feeling completely drained, even after a full night's sleep. Motivation becomes a rare commodity, and finding joy in our work becomes a real challenge. And let me tell you, that exhaustion doesn't stop at the office door. It seeps into our personal lives and relationships, like a stain that's impossible to wash out.

Another sign of burnout is a decreased sense of accomplishment. We start questioning whether the work we do actually makes a difference. It's like we're constantly falling short of our own expectations and the expectations of others. And let me tell you, that feeling of inadequacy, it's a slippery slope that leads straight to burnout.

Then there's depersonalization. This is when we start to develop a cynical attitude towards our work and the people we serve. We become numb to the pain and loss because we're constantly exposed to it. We start emotionally distancing ourselves from those we're supposed to care for, and that, my friend, is a dangerous road to walk. It hinders our ability to provide the compassionate care that's so crucial in our line of work.

But fear not, my fellow morticians, for there are practical tips and techniques to prevent and address burnout. First and foremost, we gotta set some boundaries. It's time we prioritize our own mental and emotional well-being by taking some time for ourselves. Maybe that means taking regular breaks during the day, or not working endless hours, or even refusing to bring work home with us. By respecting these boundaries, we create a healthier work-life balance that can help keep burnout at bay.

Self-care is another essential tool in our arsenal against burnout. We need to engage in activities that recharge our batteries. It could be something as simple as practicing mindfulness or meditation, getting regular exercise, or indulging in hobbies outside of work. The key is to make self-care a priority, to actively replenish our emotional reserves and build up our resilience in the face of stress.

And don't forget about seeking support. It's crucial. We need to share our experiences and concerns with our colleagues who understand the unique challenges we face. It's like having an emotional safety valve where we can let out all our frustrations and find comfort in knowing we're not alone. And let's not overlook our supervisors either. They play a vital role in addressing burnout by making sure our workloads are manageable, providing resources, and fostering a supportive environment.

Finally, we should remember that tackling burnout is an ongoing process. It requires consistent effort and self-reflection. We need to check in with ourselves regularly, evaluate our well-being, and make adjustments as necessary. Sometimes that means rethinking our goals, reassessing our priorities, and, hey, seeking professional help if we need it.

By recognizing and addressing burnout, we're not only taking care of ourselves but also creating a better work environment for our whole team. We chose this profession because it requires strength and compassion, but we can't pour from an empty cup. So let's prioritize our well-being, set those boundaries, practice self-care, and lean on each other when times get tough. Together, my friends, we can kick burnout to the curb and create a workplace that thrives with empathy and care.

Building a Supportive Team

LISTEN UP, FOLKS. I'VE got some tried-and-true strategies for building a killer team that knows how to work together like a well-oiled machine. It all starts with creating a safe space where everyone feels comfortable to speak their mind. Picture a cozy living room where you can kick back and let loose with your ideas. That's the kind of vibe we're aiming for here.

Now, let's get one thing straight - every member of this team is important. We all bring different strengths to the table, and recognizing and appreciating those strengths is key to building respect and cooperation. I mean, let's face it, our job as morticians is tough - physically and emotionally draining. But knowing that we're all in this together and that each of us plays a vital role keeps us motivated to support one another through the ups and downs.

Creating that safe space for open communication means setting some ground rules. Think active listening, no interrupting or judging, and making sure everyone gets their say. By laying out these guidelines, we create an environment where everyone feels valued and confident enough to share their thoughts and concerns. It's like building a fortress of trust and understanding.

Now, conflicts are bound to happen when you get a bunch of personalities in one room. But we can't let them fester and ruin our team spirit. The key is to address conflicts head-on, like grown-ups. Let both parties have their say, listen to their perspectives, and facilitate a respectful conversation. We're all adults here, right? We can figure this out and find solutions that actually work.

Effective communication is the glue that holds this team together. We need to encourage honest and transparent conversations, where no one feels afraid to voice their concerns or ask for help. Regular team meetings are a great way to keep the communication channels wide open. We can discuss any challenges, share updates, and remind ourselves of our shared goals. And let's not forget about using technology to stay connected outside of work. Don't worry, I'm not suggesting constant work-related texts, but having the option to reach out and lend a helping hand can make a world of difference.

But let's not forget about taking care of ourselves. We spend so much time taking care of others that we often forget about our own well-being. It's time to prioritize self-care, my friends. That means hitting the gym, taking some time for ourselves, and seeking out the mental health support we need. Because when we take care of ourselves, we can bring our A-game to this team.

Oh, and it's important to give credit where credit is due. We've got an amazing group of individuals here, and we need to acknowledge and celebrate their achievements. It's not just about boosting morale, it's about instilling pride and a sense of accomplishment. A pat on the back can go a long way, folks.

Now, building a supportive team doesn't just happen within the workplace. We've got to get out of these four walls and connect on a personal level. That means team lunches, social outings, and maybe even giving back to the community together. By strengthening our bonds outside of work, we create a support system that's got our backs no matter what.

Finally, this is an ongoing process, people. We need to constantly reassess our team dynamic and look for areas to grow. That means gathering feedback from the team, hearing out any concerns or suggestions, and making changes where needed. We're in this for the long haul, so let's keep evolving and supporting each other every step of the way.

So, in a nutshell, building a supportive team is how we'll conquer the stresses and compassion fatigue that come with our line of work. With a safe space for communication, prompt conflict resolution, and effective communication, we'll be a force to be reckoned with. And let's not forget about self-care, celebrating achievements, and those team-building activities that keep us connected outside of work. By constantly improving and nurturing our team dynamics, we create an environment that fosters growth, trust, and mutual support. Together, we'll conquer any challenge that comes our way.

Promoting Self-Care Practices

LET'S FACE IT, EMOTIONS run high in our profession. That's where mindfulness exercises swoop in like the superhero we never knew we needed. Take a deep breath and picture this: meditation and deep breathing becoming your new go-to tools for finding inner peace amidst the chaos. Sounds pretty sweet, right? I'll guide you through these practical techniques that will have you feeling as calm as a zen master.

When the demands of our profession start to weigh you down, meditation is your golden ticket to a calm mind and a break from it all. Find yourself a quiet spot, get comfy, and zero in on that breath of yours. Let intrusive thoughts fade away as the stillness takes over. Trust me, even a few minutes of meditation each day can do wonders for your overall well-being.

Do you need stress relief on the go? Look no further than deep breathing exercises. These babies can be done anytime, anywhere, and they're the ultimate convenience for those chaotic days. Inhale deeply through your nose and let that belly of yours rise, then exhale slowly through your mouth, releasing tension with each breath. Phew! It's incredible how these simple exercises can bring you moments of calm and give you the clarity and resilience to conquer anything.

Don't forget, taking care of your body is just as crucial as nurturing your mind. Regular physical activity will not only make you feel like a champ physically, but it also works wonders for your mental well-being. So, whether you fancy a brisk walk, a yoga class, or an energizing morning run, find that exercise that makes you feel alive and watch those stress levels drop while your energy soars!

Let's kick it up a notch with some holistic approaches to keep your physical well-being on point. Ever tried acupuncture, massage therapy, or aromatherapy? These practices address both physical and emotional imbalances, offering you a well-rounded approach to your own well-being. Trust me, there's nothing like a little TLC for your mind and body.

Making self-care a priority is no easy feat, my friends. But here's the thing: it's essential for our own sanity. By recognizing the impact self-care has on our well-being, we can develop strategies to make it an integral part of our daily routine. Treat your self-care activities like non-negotiable appointments with yourself that cannot be canceled or postponed. You're worth it, don't forget that!

One of my favorite ways to incorporate self-care into daily life is to create a self-care ritual. Picture this: a morning routine that starts with meditation, a healthy breakfast, and a little bit of journaling. Throughout the day, take short breaks to stretch, practice some deep breathing, or get outside and connect with nature. And to cap it all off, end your day with a relaxing ritual, whether that's a soothing bath or indulging in your favorite hobby. These rituals will help you unwind and transition into a restful sleep. Sweet dreams!

So, my fellow morticians, let's make self-care a no-brainer in our demanding lives. Mindfulness exercises, like meditation and deep breathing, are the keys to finding our inner peace and mental clarity. And don't forget about nurturing our physical well-being through exercise and holistic approaches—they'll keep us going strong physically and mentally. By making self-care an unbreakable part of our daily routine, we'll be recharged and ready to rock our work, inspiring others to do the same. Remember: self-care isn't selfish; it's the foundation for our strength and the top-notch care we provide to others.

Supporting Colleagues Through Compassion Fatigue

COMPASSION FATIGUE, man, it's like this inevitable weight that comes with being a caregiver. You're constantly exposed to all the pain and sorrow, and it starts to take a toll on your own emotional well-being. But it ain't just about us, you know? We've got a responsibility to support our colleagues through all the same struggles of compassion fatigue.

Recognizing the signs of compassion fatigue in our colleagues is huge. It shows up in all sorts of ways - less empathy, getting all irritable, just feeling emotionally wiped out. And when that fatigue sets in, man, it can make you cynical or detached from what you do. And that just tanks job satisfaction and performance. We gotta keep an eye out and show some compassion, create a space where they can let it all out, where they can express their emotions and concerns without judgment.

But it ain't just about being there for 'em, it's also about getting 'em to be there for themselves. That's where self-reflection comes in. We gotta encourage our colleagues to check in with themselves, to really think about their own emotional well-being. Maybe that's through journaling, or getting into some mindfulness exercises, or even joining support groups where they can share and reflect on their experiences. By looking inward, we can gain some insight into our own emotions and learn how to cope with compassion fatigue.

And man, providing resources is key too. We gotta give our colleagues the tools they need to handle the weight of compassion fatigue. That might mean setting up workshops or training sessions on stress management or meditation techniques. Or maybe it's about teaching 'em to set healthy boundaries. When we equip our team with the knowledge and tools to navigate their emotions, we're empowering them to take control of their own well-being.

But resilience, man, that's the secret sauce. We've gotta build up that ability to bounce back and adapt, because this field is tough. We gotta create an environment that's all about self-care, work-life balance, and open communication. Maybe that means having regular debriefing sessions or setting up emotional support networks. When we give our colleagues a chance to share their experiences, their concerns, and their successes, we're building up this awesome sense of camaraderie and a support system that's there for 'em.

And listen, the stigma around compassion fatigue? We gotta tear that down. So many caregivers feel ashamed or guilty about experiencing emotional exhaustion, like it somehow undermines their dedication to the work. But that ain't right, man. We've gotta create a culture that sees and validates the emotional challenges we face. We gotta talk about compassion fatigue openly, let everyone know it's a real thing that affects us all. If we do that, we can break down the walls that keep people from asking for help.

As morticians, we get it. We know the emotional demands of this job better than anyone. By supporting our colleagues through compassion fatigue, we're creating a workplace that puts self-care first, that acknowledges the importance of emotional well-being. When we all come together and understand each other, we see more job satisfaction, better performance, and a more compassionate approach to caregiving.

So look, supporting our colleagues through compassion fatigue, it's what we've gotta do. It's how we build a caring, resilient workplace. When we can spot the signs and offer support, when we promote self-reflection and provide resources, when we foster resilience and break down stigma - that's when we're truly addressing the unique challenges of caregiving.

From Burnout to Balance: Strategies for Sustainable Self-Care

---

The Breaking Point: When Stress Becomes Overwhelming

I remember when it all began, like a storm brewing on the horizon. Working as a mortician, I thought I had prepared myself for the constant exposure to death and grief. Little did I know, I was about to experience a turmoil that no amount of preparation could shield me from. Each day was a whirlwind of emotions, from the heartbreaking sobs of grieving families to the overwhelming sense of emptiness that clung to my every step.

As if the emotional toll wasn't enough, my body bore the scars of this profession too. The long hours spent on my feet, lugging heavy caskets and dealing with dangerous chemicals, took their toll on me. Chronic back pain became my unwelcome companion, and exhaustion became the norm. Sleep became elusive as my mind replayed the haunting images and sounds of death, infecting every waking moment.

The stress seeped into every corner of my life, poisoning my relationships. My loved ones had no idea how heavy the burden on my shoulders truly was, how it shackled me to a state of detachment and withdrawal. Their frustration grew as I became a distant figure, unable to fully engage in any moment. Even my significant other, once my rock, slipped through my grasp as our relationship crumbled under the weight of my stress.

There was one moment that stands out in my memory, the breaking point that tore through the fragile fabric of my sanity. It was an exceptionally grueling week, with death after death and complex funeral arrangements. My body screamed in agony, my mind raced, and suddenly, it all became too much. The embalming room became my sanctuary of tears, a sacred space where I could release the weight of my anguish in uncontrollable sobs.

That moment of despair shook me awake. I knew something had to change. I couldn't continue down this path of self-destruction. My physical and mental health were hanging by a thread, and I had to find a way to nurture myself. It was a long-overdue realization that I couldn't pour from an empty cup. My journey of self-care had to begin if I wanted to continue doing the work that set my soul on fire.

Through this journey, I discovered the warning signs that signaled I was nearing the edge. The red flags waved boldly, imploring me to take heed. Physical symptoms like chronic fatigue, insomnia, and the persistent ache in my back were calls for a respite. The strain on my relationships acted as an alarm, signaling that I had put my own needs on the backburner for far too long.

So, I embarked on a path of self-care, seeking solace in those moments that brought me joy and peace. I found refuge in the stillness of meditation, a lifeline to quiet my racing thoughts and find balance amidst the chaos. Physical exercise became a vital release, a way to move my body and release those much-needed endorphins. And perhaps most importantly, I learned how to set boundaries and say no when the weight of the world threatened to consume me. It was a lesson steeped in adversity, but one that was imperative for my well-being.

Through my own story, I hope to shine a light on the reality of the breaking point we face as morticians and the urgency of self-care. We must tend to our own souls so that we can continue to provide compassion and support to those in need. By recognizing the warning signs and prioritizing self-care, we can find balance between the demands of our careers and personal lives. Remember, self-care is not a luxury; it's a necessity for survival in the demanding world of mortuary work.

Unmasking Compassion Fatigue: The Hidden Toll of Caring

I'VE ALWAYS BEEN A mortician, a person who takes care of others during their darkest times. It's a job that requires me to be there for families when they're grieving, guiding them through the heart-wrenching process of saying goodbye to their loved ones. And though there's a certain satisfaction that comes from being able to bring some comfort and support to those who need it, there's also a hidden toll that comes with the territory.

Compassion fatigue is this silent killer in the mortuary profession. It sneaks up on you, slowly suffocating your ability to provide true compassion. In this little story, I'm going to take off the mask we all wear and dive into the brutal reality of compassion fatigue, how it slowly builds up over time, and the effect it can have on our own well-being.

One particular encounter sticks out in my memory, forever reminding me of the cost of compassion fatigue. A mother, devastated and broken, came to me when she lost her teenage son to a tragic accident. She poured her heart out, sharing stories and memories of her vibrant and promising child. Her grief weighed on me like an anchor, sinking deep into my soul. I absorbed her pain, feeling it as if it were my own. Hours later, as I stood there at the funeral service, watching her collapse in a sea of tears, a wave of helplessness washed over me. The emotional toll of carrying her burden had left me empty, my own capacity for compassion drained.

This encounter wasn't an isolated incident. Over the years, I've noticed patterns in my own emotional well-being. Each time I encountered a grieving family, a residue of pain would accumulate within me. Their sorrow would weigh heavy on my heart, seeping into the core of my being. It became harder to separate their pain from my own, to keep my emotions compartmentalized.

Research shows that those of us in helping professions, like morticians, are particularly susceptible to compassion fatigue. We witness grief in its purest form, day in and day out, seeing the devastating impact of loss on families. Our empathy and desire to support leave us vulnerable to the infectious power of grief. Over time, this constant exposure can lead to emotional exhaustion, loss of empathy, and a decline in our sense of self-worth.

But what causes this compassion fatigue? It's a complex mix of factors that all contribute to the toll it takes on us. Long hours, heavy workloads, and the relentless pressure to always be there for families in need wear down our emotional resilience. It becomes harder to set boundaries as we dedicate every moment to others. Balancing our professional responsibilities with our personal lives creates a constant state of tension, making the emotional toll even worse.

Furthermore, the mortuary profession often demands silence, expects us to bury our own vulnerabilities and put on a facade of strength. We're supposed to be unwavering pillars of support for those who come to us seeking comfort, our own struggles hidden beneath a mask of professionalism. This pressure to hide our emotions, to bear others' burdens without showing any cracks, only amplifies the toll of compassion fatigue on our well-being.

But we must recognize that compassion fatigue isn't a sign of weakness; it's a reflection of our capacity for empathy and care. To continue providing compassion to those in need, we must first acknowledge and address our own emotional well-being. That starts with uncovering the hidden toll of caring and finding ways to prevent compassion fatigue from overwhelming our lives.

Redefining Boundaries: Setting Limits for Self-Care

WHEN I FIRST STEPPED foot into the world of mortuary profession, I was immediately enchanted by the idea of being there for others during their most vulnerable moments. The thought of providing compassion and support to those in need fueled my every step. I was convinced that my dedication and empathy would be enough to sustain me emotionally. But as days turned into weeks, and weeks turned into months, I began to realize that I was neglecting my own needs in the process. The heavy weight of long hours, constantly being exposed to grief, and the overwhelming responsibility I carried began to wear me down, both mentally and physically.

It was during one particularly arduous case that I hit my breaking point. Exhaustion had taken hold of me, as I had been working tirelessly for days on end, barely finding the time to nourish my body or rest my weary eyes. The grief that engulfed the air felt like a vice around my chest, suffocating me with its intensity. In that moment, I knew that something had to change. I had to redefine my boundaries and set limits for the sake of my own well-being.

Prioritizing my own self-care became my top priority. I started to carve out moments of respite throughout the day, even if it meant stealing a few minutes to take a brisk walk or engage in deep breathing exercises. Nature became my sanctuary, so I would often escape to a nearby park during my lunch break, allowing myself to disconnect from the demands of work and recharge in the embrace of fresh air and sunlight.

But establishing boundaries with clients and coworkers was just as crucial. I had to learn to communicate my availability and limitations upfront, making it clear that I needed time for myself in order to maintain my own well-being. It wasn't easy at first, for I didn't want to disappoint or let anyone down. Yet, I soon came to realize that by setting these boundaries, I was actually enhancing the quality of care I could provide. By allowing myself the space to recharge, I was able to show up fully present and attentive when I was at work.

Perhaps the most transformative aspect of redefining my boundaries was learning to say no without guilt. In the realm of mortuary profession, there is often an expectation of being available around the clock, no matter the circumstances. The pressure to be there for others at any given moment can be overwhelming. But I came to a profound understanding that I couldn't pour from an empty cup. Saying no wasn't a reflection of my dedication or compassion; it was a reflection of my own self-awareness and commitment to prioritizing my well-being.

In my journey of redefining boundaries and setting limits for self-care, I also unearthed the profound importance of self-compassion. It's so easy to be hard on ourselves, to push through exhaustion and sacrifice our own needs for the sake of others. However, true compassion begins within ourselves. I learned that it was perfectly okay to prioritize my own well-being, to take breaks when needed, and to ask for help when I felt overwhelmed.

Through this transformative process, I discovered a renewed sense of balance and fulfillment in my mortuary career. By reshaping my relationship with work and making self-care a non-negotiable priority, I was able to show up as the best version of myself - for both my clients and my coworkers. It became clear to me that by taking care of myself, I was ultimately providing better care for others.

Undoubtedly, there will always be moments of intense grief and emotional exhaustion in the mortuary profession. That is the nature of the work we do. But by redefining boundaries and setting limits for self-care, I have found a way to navigate these challenges with grace and resilience. I now understand that self-care is not a luxury, but an absolute necessity - a vital component of maintaining a healthy and fulfilling career in the mortuary profession.

The journey of redefining boundaries and setting limits for self-care is a deeply personal and transformative one. It requires a commitment to oneself, a willingness to prioritize self-care, and the courage to confidently say no when necessary. By reshaping your relationship with work, establishing clear boundaries, and prioritizing self-compassion, you'll find a renewed sense of balance, fulfillment, and longevity in your mortuary career. Remember, you cannot pour from an empty cup, and by taking care of yourself, you will be better equipped to care for others.

Finding Light in the Darkness: Cultivating Resilience

ONE OF THE MOST POWERFUL strategies I've found is practicing gratitude. I know, it sounds strange to focus on what we're grateful for when we're facing such heartache and loss. But believe me, it's like a lifeline that keeps us afloat when we feel like we're sinking under the weight of grief. I remember this one time when a young child had passed away, and the sorrow was overwhelming. In those moments, I turned to my gratitude journal. Every day, I would write down three things I was grateful for. It could be as simple as a warm cup of tea or the comforting embrace of a loved one. By shifting my focus onto these moments of light, I realized that even in the darkest times, there's still some beauty to be found.

Another crucial aspect of finding resilience in this profession is seeking support from fellow morticians. We all carry this heavy load of grief, and even though our experiences may be different, there's this shared understanding between us. It's like finding solace in talking to someone who truly gets it. Whether it's those informal chats during breaks or joining professional organizations, having a community of like-minded individuals can make a world of difference in how we cope with the emotional rollercoaster of our work.

But sometimes, we need more than just support from within our profession. That's where external resources come in. Therapy and counseling have been absolute game-changers for me in finding resilience. Talking to a professional who knows how to navigate the complexities of grief can provide a safe space to process our emotions and develop coping mechanisms. And don't underestimate the power of support groups or online forums, where you can hear from others who have gone through similar experiences. It helps to know we're not alone in this struggle.

Now, let me tell you about this one incident that will forever be etched in my memory. It was the loss of a close friend and colleague, and the grief that settled among us was suffocating. I honestly didn't know how I could bounce back from such a profound loss. That's when I turned to art as therapy. Painting and drawing became my refuge, my way of expressing all that weight of grief when words just couldn't do it justice. Through those brush strokes and pencil marks, I could release some of that sorrow and find a glimmer of hope and resilience.

But let me be real with you. Building resilience doesn't happen overnight. It requires a commitment to our own well-being. Self-care is key to maintaining our emotional stamina. We need to engage in activities that bring us joy and nourish our souls. It could be something as simple as taking a quiet walk in nature or listening to music that lifts our spirits. And hey, let's not forget about mindfulness practices that help ground us. We have to prioritize our own well-being if we want to stay strong and resilient in our work as morticians.

Through this journey, I've come to realize that resilience isn't about erasing the pain or pretending it's not there. It's about finding those bright spots in the darkness. It's about embracing moments of grace and beauty that still exist, even in the midst of profound grief. By practicing gratitude, seeking support, using therapeutic outlets, and taking care of ourselves, we can navigate the emotional rollercoasters of our profession and come out stronger and more resilient.

So as we continue on this path of mortuary work, let's remember that our ability to bring light to grieving families depends on our own ability to find that light within ourselves. We are the ones who hold compassion and solace in the darkest of times, and by nurturing our resilience, we can continue to be beacons of hope for those who need it most.

Thriving, Not Just Surviving: Nurturing Your Well-Being

WHEN I FIRST STEPPED foot into the world of mortuary science, I was hit with a tidal wave of challenges that felt impossible to conquer. The never-ending exposure to grief and loss can wear down even the strongest of souls, and I soon found myself clinging to the edge of burnout, emotionally drained and ready to crumble. It was in the midst of this personal crisis that I realized I had to put myself first in order to continue helping those in need.

So, I took the first step on this journey of self-discovery by diving into self-reflection exercises. Each day, I carved out time to simply sit and be with my own thoughts and emotions. I allowed myself to fully experience the ups and downs that surged within me, without judging or pushing them aside. Through this practice, I learned just how important it was to acknowledge and process my own grief, and to establish clear boundaries to protect my own emotional well-being.

But self-reflection wasn't the only tool in my arsenal; I also started incorporating self-care rituals into my daily routine. Yoga, meditation, and journaling became my lifelines, offering me moments of peace in the midst of the chaos that defined my profession. These practices not only helped me to unwind and find balance, but they also instilled a sense of inner strength and resilience. I discovered that by taking care of myself, I could better care for others.

And then came the unexpected twist—I decided to actively seek out joy in my work. It may sound counterintuitive, finding happiness amidst the sadness, but I firmly believe that it's crucial for our own well-being and the well-being of those we serve. I made a conscious effort to create connections and find beauty even in the darkest moments. Whether it was offering a comforting word to a grieving family or creating a peaceful atmosphere in the viewing room, I sought out opportunities to infuse joy into my work. And let me tell you, witnessing the transformative power of compassion and empathy first-hand was nothing short of awe-inspiring.

As I continued down this path of self-discovery and self-care, I couldn't help but notice a remarkable shift within me. The weight of my profession no longer felt crushing; instead,

I felt empowered and inspired to make a real difference. Prioritizing my own well-being had not only allowed me to thrive as a mortician, but it had also given me a more fulfilling and sustainable career.

So, my message to all my fellow mortuary professionals is this: survival isn't enough—we deserve to thrive. Through self-reflection exercises, the incorporation of self-care rituals, and the intentional cultivation of joy in our work, we can put ourselves first and create a truly fulfilling and sustainable career in this field. I hope that by sharing my own journey of self-discovery, you'll find the inspiration to embrace these transformative practices and embark on your own path towards thriving in the mortuary profession.

Reflecting on Resilience: Real-Life Stories and Testimonials

A Glimpse Behind the Veil

As a mortician, let me tell you, my fascination with death goes way beyond your average curiosity. Growing up, I found comfort in cemeteries, finding this odd sense of peace amid the tombstones and the stories they held. And that fascination? Yeah, it led me down a path that most people would never dare to take.

Embalmings, man, they're this mystifying yet hauntingly beautiful process. It's like an art form, you know? These delicate hands, they delicately manipulate the deceased. Every detail, from how the body is positioned to the expression on their face, is carefully crafted to provide some solace to the grieving loved ones left behind.

But there's more to being a mortician than just mastering embalming techniques. We also take on the role of professional organizers, like conductors leading an orchestra. We gotta make sure that the deceased is honored and remembered in the most fitting way possible. And trust me, that's no easy feat. We have to understand cultural traditions, respect personal preferences, and most importantly, handle some seriously tough situations with grace and compassion.

But let me tell you a little secret about us morticians. Behind the scenes, we're faced with a whole bunch of challenges. There's something called compassion fatigue, and it ain't just something that affects healthcare professionals. Nope, it weighs heavy on us too. Constantly witnessing grief and loss, man, it takes a toll on our mental and physical well-being.

And you know what? It's not uncommon for us morticians to have moments where we feel real vulnerable, you know? Dealing with death all the time, it forces us to look inwards and really think about how fragile life is. It's a sobering reminder to appreciate each moment we have on this earth and to find solace in the connections and relationships that keep us going.

But let me tell you something. We wouldn't survive in this line of work without a strong support system. We find solace in our colleagues, forming bonds that go beyond just the usual workplace camaraderie. These connections give us a safe space to share our experiences and find comfort in others who understand the unique challenges we face.

And self-care? Man, that's a must in this line of work. We gotta learn how to prioritize ourselves, how to cope with the emotional toll. That means practicing mindfulness, seeking therapy if we need it, doing whatever it takes to prevent burnout, man. 'Cause if we don't take care of ourselves, how can we take care of others?

Oh, and finding balance? Yeah, that's crucial too. We gotta learn how to navigate the tricky waters of being caregivers while also caring for ourselves. It means setting boundaries, recognizing the early signs of burnout, and being damn willing to ask for help when we need it.

Through all my experiences in this funeral industry, I've come to appreciate the intricate and often misunderstood aspects of this profession. It's this world filled with mystery, but oh man, does it hold beauty and grace. The resilience it takes to not only survive but thrive in this demanding role, it's a testament to the unwavering dedication of us morticians.

The Light in the Darkness

YOU KNOW, AS A MORTICIAN, I'm pretty acquainted with all the dark and gloomy stuff that comes with death. It's a whole world filled with sadness, heartache, and pain, and most folks don't realize just how heavy it can be unless they've walked this path themselves. But, here's the twist, my friend – amidst all that darkness, there's a glimmer of light waiting to be discovered.

You might be wondering how in the heck we morticians manage to deal with death day in and day out without going nuts. Well, let me tell ya, it ain't a walk in the park. But it's a calling we've chosen, driven by an overwhelming sense of compassion and a burning desire to bring comfort to those who need it most.

Now, one thing we morticians swear by for keeping our heads above water is self-care. Sounds simple, right? But it's crucial in a gig where grief and loss can pile up faster than dirty laundry. For me, it's about recognizing and honoring my own emotions. It's easy to shut down and numb yourself to it all, but letting myself feel and work through my own grief is key to avoiding a complete meltdown.

There's something magical about the sense of community among us morticians, too. This line of work binds us together in a way nothing else can. We find solace in support groups where we can let it all out and talk about the struggles we face. It's like therapy, but with people who truly get it. We vent, we seek advice, and we draw strength from each other's stories. Through these connections, we learn that we're not alone, that others face the same battles, and that hope never truly dies.

And hey, don't knock the power of meditation and mindfulness. That's another secret weapon us morticians use to find some light in the darkness. By giving ourselves a break and honing in on the present moment, we can untangle the mess in our heads and find some much-needed peace. Taking a deep breath and slowing down, it gives us the strength to keep going, to be there for the grieving, and to see purpose in what we do.

But here's something you might not have thought of – art. Yeah, that's right. Painting, writing, playing music – all those creative outlets help us morticians salvage some sanity. It's a way to give a voice to our emotions, to interpret the chaos and turn it into something tangible. And you know what?

Art can find beauty even in the darkest moments. It becomes our way of bearing witness to the things we've experienced.

Nature, my friend, is another refuge we morticians seek when we need a break from the intensity of our job. Taking a stroll in the woods, sitting by the shore, or tending to a garden – it lets us recharge and regain some perspective. It reminds us that life keeps moving, that there's something bigger than all the sorrow we see day in and day out.

Last but not least, finding balance is absolutely crucial for any mortician looking to keep their sanity intact. Yeah, our work can easily consume us, but we've gotta remember that we're more than just the grim reaper's buddies. Hobbies, spending time with loved ones, finding joy outside of work – those are all ingredients in the recipe for a fulfilling life. By nurturing all the other parts of ourselves, we build up resilience that helps us weather the storms that come our way.

Joining the ranks of morticians who've learned to find light in the darkness is a journey of strength, kindness, and self-discovery. It's a testament to how we humans can adapt and grow even when faced with overwhelming challenges. So, my friend, through self-care, community support, mindfulness, artistic expression, soaking in nature, and striking a balance, we morticians can walk this path with compassion and grace. In doing so, we listen to the tales of grief, offer solace in times of despair, and ultimately, find meaning and purpose in a world touched by death.

Lighting the Path for Others

LET ME REINTRODUCE you to Sarah Turner, a mortician who has truly paved the way for others in our field. Like many of us, Sarah initially entered the funeral industry fueled by compassion and a genuine desire to help people during their darkest times. But as the years went by, the weight of the emotional toll started to drag her down. Constant exposure to grief and loss left her feeling drained and empty. In the midst of her own struggle with compassion fatigue, Sarah realized she had to find a way to take care of herself so she could continue being there for others.

And so, Sarah's journey toward self-care and resilience began with a simple step - admitting her limitations and reaching out for support. She sought out colleagues who had felt the same way and found solace in sharing their experiences. They formed a support group where they could openly discuss their challenges and offer each other the encouragement and understanding they desperately needed. Through this camaraderie, Sarah felt less isolated and reminded herself that she wasn't alone in her struggles.

But Sarah's determination didn't stop there. She saw the need for formalized support and resources specifically tailored to morticians dealing with stress and compassion fatigue. With a burning passion to make a difference, she advocated for the creation of support programs within funeral organizations. She tirelessly wrote articles, gave presentations, and fought for change, all with the goal of spreading awareness about the importance of self-care in our field.

And eventually, Sarah's efforts paid off. Support programs were established, providing counseling, workshops, and resources for morticians. These initiatives not only helped individuals cope with the emotional toll of their work but also fostered a culture of self-care within our profession. Sarah had become a beacon of light, illuminating a path for others to follow in the funeral industry.

Another mortician who has become an inspiration and support figure in our field is Jonathan Ramirez. Jonathan's journey toward self-care started after he experienced burnout firsthand. Pushing himself to the limit, working tirelessly without breaks - both his body and mind began to suffer. He realized that if he wanted to continue helping others, he had to prioritize taking care of himself.

Jonathan's approach to self-care was multi-faceted, encompassing physical, emotional, and spiritual practices. He started focusing on regular exercise, recognizing the importance of keeping his body in shape to withstand the physical strain of our work. Jonathan also made a conscious effort to incorporate mindfulness and meditation into his daily routine, finding moments of peace within the chaos. And to truly address the emotional toll, he sought therapy, allowing himself to process the emotions that were often suppressed.

But Jonathan didn't keep his newfound knowledge and practices to himself. Like Sarah, he felt an undeniable call to share his experiences and the tools he had discovered with others. Jonathan began offering workshops and training sessions specifically designed for morticians, teaching them not only self-care techniques but also the significance of setting boundaries and prioritizing their well-being.

Through his workshops, Jonathan demonstrated the power of vulnerability and the strength it takes to acknowledge and address our struggles. He encouraged open and honest conversations within the mortician community, smashing the stigma associated with seeking help. Jonathan's approach to self-care was holistic, reminding his colleagues that they weren't just professionals but individuals deserving of care and compassion.

Sarah Turner and Jonathan Ramirez are just two shining examples of the many morticians who have become beacons of light for others in our profession. Through their personal journeys, they have shown us that it's possible to not only survive but thrive despite the stress and fatigue. Their stories serve as reminders that self-care isn't a luxury but a necessity for anyone working in a demanding and emotionally taxing industry like ours.

As I continue navigating the world of self-care and resilience in the funeral industry, I am continuously inspired by individuals like Sarah and Jonathan. They've taken their own struggles and transformed them into opportunities for growth and support. Their stories remind me that I'm not alone on this journey, and they fill me with hope that together, we can create a culture of self-care within our mortician community.

Building a Brighter Future: The Path Forward

Embracing Change: The Power of Adaptability

I have to admit, change has always been a tough pill for me to swallow. It's like this force that sneaks up on you, demanding that you let go of what's comfortable and familiar. And man, do we love our routines, don't we? We cling to them for dear life, afraid to venture into the great unknown. But as a mortician, I've come to realize that resisting change is like fighting against the tide - it's exhausting and ultimately futile.

I'll never forget those early years of being a mortician, when I thought I had it all figured out. I had learned the tried and true methods, and I naively believed that they would carry me through my entire career. But boy, was I wrong. The world around me was shifting, and the funeral industry was no exception. Families wanted more personalized services, cremations were gaining popularity, and technology was revolutionizing how we communicated with our clients. It was enough to make any traditional mortician break out in a cold sweat.

So there I was, standing at a crossroads, unsure of which path to take. Should I stick with the old ways, even if it meant burning out and feeling dissatisfied? Or should I take a leap of faith and embrace the winds of change, knowing that it could lead to growth and innovation in my profession?

I chose change. And let me tell you, it was no walk in the park. I stumbled along the way, grappling with doubt and uncertainty. But with each stumble, I learned something valuable about the power of adaptability. It was during a time when the funeral industry was experiencing a seismic shift in how we approached funeral services that a profound realization struck me.

I was at a service unlike any I had seen before. Instead of the usual somber atmosphere, there was a palpable sense of celebration in the air. The family had requested a joyous celebration of their loved one's life, with vibrant colors, lively music, and stories that brought laughter instead of tears. And you know what? It worked. In that moment, surrounded by laughter and tears of joy, I realized that change had given us the freedom to break free from the confines of tradition. We were able to create an experience that truly honored the spirit of the departed and brought comfort to those left behind.

From that moment on, I understood that adaptability isn't just about surviving in a changing world. It's about thriving in it. It's about having the courage to let go of the old ways and embrace new possibilities. Instead of viewing change as a threat, I started seeing it as an opportunity for growth and reinvention.

So, if you're a mortician like me, wondering how to navigate the treacherous waters of change, here are a few tips I've picked up along the way:

1. Nurture a growth mindset: Believe that you can learn and grow through challenges. Embrace setbacks as opportunities for self-reflection and improvement.

2. Keep an open mind: Be curious about new ideas and approaches, even if they challenge your old ways of doing things. Embrace the unknown and seek out chances to expand your knowledge and skills.

3. Encourage innovation: Create an environment that fosters creativity and experimentation. Let your colleagues and staff members know that their ideas are valued.

4. Stay informed: Attend conferences, workshops, and seminars that focus on the latest trends and advancements in the funeral industry. Be aware of emerging technologies and practices.

5. Build a support network: Surround yourself with fellow morticians who share your passion for the industry. Lean on them for support, guidance, and inspiration.

Embracing change is no easy task. It takes guts, resilience, and a willingness to let go of what no longer serves us. But trust me, it's worth it. By embracing change, we have the power to transform not only ourselves, but also the very landscape of our profession. It's a wild ride, but hey, life would be pretty boring without a few twists and turns, right?

Nurturing Resilience: Bouncing Back From Adversity

LET ME TAKE YOU ON a journey through the world of resilience, my friend. As a mortician, I've faced my fair share of challenges that have put my resilience to the ultimate test. And let me tell you, resilience is not just something you're born with or not. It's a quality that can be nurtured and grown, like a beautiful flower in a field of adversity.

But before we dive into the depths of resilience, we must acknowledge the hardships that we morticians face. Movies and TV shows may give you a glimpse of our work, but they don't capture the full story. The long hours, the physical and emotional toll, the constant bombardment of trauma - it all takes a toll on our well-being. We're constantly exposed to grief and death, and it's all too easy to lose ourselves in the process. The weight of our own emotions can be overwhelming while we try to provide comfort to others. It's a delicate dance that requires unwavering resilience.

Resilience, my friend, is not just about bouncing back from tough situations. It's about learning to adapt, to grow, and to thrive in the face of adversity. Some folks may have a natural knack for resilience, but it's not something that can't be learned. With practice and dedication, we can cultivate the strength within us to overcome even the most harrowing experiences.

Let me share a story from my own journey to show you the power of resilience. Early in my career, I was faced with a heart-wrenching case. A young child had tragically lost their life in a car accident, and the family was shattered. As I prepared the child for their final journey, the weight of the tragedy bore down on me. The room was suffused with grief and sorrow, palpable enough to touch.

It was in that moment that I truly understood the importance of resilience. I had a choice to make - to let the emotional weight break me or to rise above it. And you know what? I chose to rise. I tapped into the deep well of strength within me and became a compassionate presence for that grieving family. I listened to their stories, finding ways to honor their child's life. It was through resilience that I not only survived that difficult situation but provided the support that was desperately needed.

That story is just a single thread in the intricate tapestry of moments where morticians must summon their resilience. Each day brings new challenges, but it's through those challenges that we grow stronger, both as individuals and professionals.

So how can we build and nurture resilience in our lives? Well, my friend, self-care is key. It's easy to forget about our own well-being when we're constantly taking care of others. But we must carve out time for ourselves - to tend to our physical, emotional, and mental health. Self-care comes in many forms, and it's a personal journey for each of us. For me, it means finding solace in nature, indulging in creative hobbies, and surrounding myself with a supportive network of loved ones. Maybe for you, it's meditation, exercise, or seeking professional help. Whatever it is, make it a regular part of your life.

And speaking of support, we can't underestimate the power of a strong support system. Surround yourself with people who understand the unique challenges we face as morticians. They'll be the ones to lend a listening ear, to provide emotional support when we need it most. Having a safe space to express our own emotions and vulnerabilities is essential. It's our refuge in a stormy world.

But that's not all, my friend. We must also reframe our mindset and adopt a positive outlook. It's easy to fall into a pit of negativity when we're constantly surrounded by grief and loss. But by focusing on the positive aspects of our work, like the ability to bring solace and closure to devastated families, we can find strength in our purpose. It's a mindset shift, my friend, and it can make all the difference.

As I reflect on my own journey, as well as the experiences of my fellow morticians, I've come to realize that resilience is not a destination. It's a never-ending process of self-reflection, adaptation, and growth. We must intentionally nurture our resilience, my friend, to face any challenge that comes our way.

Life as a mortician is no walk in the park. It's a path riddled with adversity. But with the right mindset, the support of our loved ones, and a commitment to self-care, we can triumph over any obstacle. Let's build a foundation of strength and resilience together, not just for ourselves, but for the families we serve and for the well-being of our noble profession.

Finding Balance: Prioritizing Self-Care in a Demanding Profession

GUYS, LET ME TELL YOU something - being a mortician ain't a walk in the park. We're constantly surrounded by death and grief, day in and day out. Our job demands long hours and tasks that really take a toll on our emotions. It's so easy to get caught up in the craziness and forget about ourselves. But listen up, just like any other profession, self-care is key for our sanity.

I'll never forget the time I hit rock bottom. It was one of those weeks where funeral after funeral lined up, and I couldn't catch a decent night's sleep because I was too busy tending to grieving families. I was completely consumed by my work, always putting others first. But man, as the days turned into weeks, and the weeks turned into months, I felt myself crashing and burning. Physically and emotionally, I was running on empty. I had totally lost sight of taking care of myself.

It was only when a fellow mortician clocked on to the toll it was all taking on me that I finally woke up. She saw right through my facade and shared her own horror stories of burnout and compassion fatigue. I swear, it was like a little switch flicked in my head. It hit me - if I don't start looking after myself, how on earth can I even begin to take care of others? I needed to find some balance, pronto.

Now, one crucial component of finding balance is making time for self-care. We're always putting everyone else's needs first, be it family, friends, or our clients. But hey, we need to recharge too, man. It can be as simple as going for a walk in the park, indulging in a hobby that lights us up inside, or just chilling alone and reflecting in peace and quiet. In this chapter, I'll hook you up with some practical tips on how to squeeze self-care into our daily lives, even with all the crazy demands of our job.

But wait, there's more - we have to talk about setting boundaries, my friends. Our work has this sneaky habit of invading every corner of our personal lives. The line between work and play becomes blurred, and that's when we get emotionally burnt out. That's why we have to lay down some solid boundaries, ya know. Knowing when to say no, passing off some tasks to others, and leaning on our colleagues and loved ones for support can make all the difference. Boundaries create space for ourselves so that our work can't swallow us whole.

And get this, we can't ignore the psychological and emotional toll our profession takes on us. Dealing with death and grief all the time can suck the empathy and compassion right outta us. It's called compassion fatigue, folks, and recognizing the signs is crucial. But hey, not to worry, I've got your back. I'll dish out some practical strategies and tools to combat and prevent compassion fatigue so we can keep doing what we do best - taking care of our clients.

You, the Mortician: A Journey of Compassion and Strength

The Mortician's Calling

You know, when I was growing up, death seemed to hold this strange fascination for me. While everyone else got all freaked out by it, I found myself strangely drawn to it. It's like death whispered secrets in my ear, you know? It's like it wanted me to be its keeper or something. As a kid, I spent hours in cemeteries, reading the names on the tombstones and trying to imagine the stories hidden beneath them. Little did I know, those moments were shaping my future as a mortician. Crazy, right?

As I got older, that pull towards the world of the dead just kept getting stronger. So, I enrolled in mortuary school, eager to learn all the ins and outs of handling deceased bodies and comforting grieving families. Let me tell you, those years were eye-opening. I realized that being a mortician doesn't just mean taking care of physical remains. It means being a guardian of memories, a healer for the brokenhearted, and a guide through the storm of grief.

The first time I walked into a funeral home as a newly licensed mortician, I felt the weight of my calling settle on my shoulders like a ton of bricks. The air was thick with reverence and sorrow. Families were huddled together, their red eyes and heavy hearts telling the story of sleepless nights and unbearable pain. And there I was, expected to bring them solace and strength.

In this part of the story, we'll explore just how complex our role as morticians is. We'll dive deep into the emotional toll it takes on us and the struggle to balance taking care of others with taking care of ourselves.

Being a mortician is a sacred bond between life and death, you know? We get to witness the vulnerability and rawness of grief firsthand. We hold space for people to express their pain and walk with them through the darkest of times. It's an honor, really. But with that honor comes the knowledge that we can get overwhelmed by it all. Compassion fatigue is always lurking, ready to take hold if we don't make sure to take care of ourselves.

In the quietness of the embalming room, I find peace in the precision of my work. It's like a dance, you know? Balancing preservation of the body with honoring the spirit of the deceased. Every cut, every stitch, is an act of reverence. That's when I truly feel the weight of my role.

Death has this way of wiping away all the little distractions in life. When grief is present, judgments and indifference just fade away. Compassion becomes our guiding light, leading us through the storm of loss. We hold the hands of the grieving, listen to their stories, and offer them whatever small comfort we can.

But beneath the surface, our own emotions are swirling around like a tempest. We witness so much pain and heartbreak, and it seeps into our very being. Sometimes it's hard to know where empathy ends and emotional exhaustion begins. We have to remain strong for others, even when we're carrying our own burdens.

Compassion fatigue is like this sneaky little devil, always waiting to pounce on us when we're vulnerable. The very thing that drives us to help others can become our biggest enemy. It's a tightrope walk, really. Trying to show we care without getting overwhelmed.

That's why self-care is so important in our profession. It's not a luxury; it's a necessity. When our job demands so much of us, we have to take breaks and take care of ourselves. We need moments of solitude, support from loved ones, and practices that rejuvenate our spirits.

Let me tell you, being a mortician is not for the faint of heart. It takes an intense amount of compassion, strength, and dedication to serve others in such a vulnerable time. It's a calling that requires our utmost attention and care. In this part of the story, we're going to dig deep into the heart of our role, exploring the profoundness of our purpose and the weight of our responsibility. Get ready, my friend, because the path of a mortician is not for the timid – it's a journey that will change your life forever.

Embracing Darkness, Illuminating Life

YOU KNOW, BEING A MORTICIAN, my days are just filled to the brim with death. It's like I'm constantly surrounded by darkness, with reminders of how fragile life really is. I mean, I get to see firsthand just how temporary everything is, how we all have an expiration date. But you know what's crazy? In the midst of all that gloom and doom, I've actually found this incredible sense of purpose and this ability to appreciate life in a way I never thought possible.

There was this one time, early on in my career, when I had to prepare the body of this young woman who had died in a terrible car accident. As I was gently washing her lifeless body, it hit me like a ton of bricks. The beauty and fragility of it all. I mean, every little curve of her face, every single strand of hair, it was like this incredible masterpiece. And right then and there, I realized just how precious life really is. How every breath, every moment... it all matters.

That moment has stayed with me ever since. It's like each new body I see is this stark reminder that our time here is so limited, and we've got to make the absolute most of it. Yeah, it sounds morbid, but death has become this intense catalyst for embracing life. It's like this constant nudge, reminding me to seize every opportunity for joy, connection, and growth.

Let me tell you about this one person who really left a mark on me. I had to prepare the body of this elderly gentleman who had lived a long and fulfilling life. And as I was dressing him, I couldn't help but get lost in the lines on his face and the wrinkles on his hands. It was like they were telling these incredible stories. And in that moment, I realized that his death wasn't the end, but a celebration of a life well lived.

Man, after his funeral, I just couldn't stop reflecting on what he had unknowingly taught me. Life isn't just about how long we're here, you know? It's about the experiences we gather along the way, the richness of it all. His death showed me the importance of living fully, of grabbing every chance to grow and connect. He inspired me to write my own story with intention and purpose.

Sure, being a mortician can be tough. I've seen countless heart-wrenching goodbyes and the weight of loss carried by loved ones. But you know what? I've also seen resilience, strength, and this amazing ability of the human spirit to find joy in even the darkest moments. It's this perfect balance between light and dark that drives me to help others navigate their own journeys of grief and self-care.

Every day, I try to create a safe space for grief and healing. I encourage people to really embrace their emotions, to dance with the darkness instead of hiding from it. Trust me, denying that darkness does no good. Embracing the somberness of death is what helps us truly appreciate life's fragility and beauty.

In the face of death, I've learned the power of being present. It's like witnessing the finality of life has taught me to treasure the present moment and the people I share it with.

Something as simple as taking a breath is no longer taken for granted. Each inhale and exhale is a reminder of how precious life is. So I make it my mission to fill every single day with love, gratitude, and a commitment to make a difference in the lives of others.

Being a mortician isn't just a job, you know? It's this calling, this deep understanding of the human experience. It's this delicate dance between darkness and light, grief and healing. But embracing that darkness has given me the power to illuminate life. To help those who have passed on as well as those who are still here.

In the midst of all that death's darkness, I've discovered the incredible power of embracing life. Every single day, I'm reminded of how sacred the human experience truly is, how fleeting our time here really is. And through my work as a mortician, I've made it my purpose to help others navigate their grief, find meaning in the face of loss, and cherish every single breath.

Behind Closed Doors: The Mortician's Secrets

WALKING INTO THE DIMLY lit embalming room is like stepping into another world. It's a place where time slows down and the noise of the outside world fades into nothingness. The air is heavy with whispered conversations and the sterile scent of disinfectant. Standing in the center of the room is the embalming table, the epicenter of the magic that happens here.

As a mortician, my job is to preserve the body of the deceased, to ensure they are presented to their loved ones in a way that pays homage to their memory. It's not a job for the faint-hearted. It requires precision, steady hands, and an unwavering commitment to the deceased. Each incision, every careful movement is done with utmost care, cleansing and disinfecting the body to protect it from decomposition.

I begin the embalming process with a gentle washing of the body. It's a ritual soaked in symbolism and respect. As the water flows over the skin, it carries away more than just physical impurities. It seems to wash away the weight of grief and sadness, allowing the deceased to be reborn in the eyes of their loved ones. Every nook and cranny is meticulously cleaned, a tribute to the unique beauty that once graced this person's life.

Next comes the delicate process of arterial embalming. It's a dance of fluid and life, as I inject a specially formulated embalming fluid into the body through the circulatory system. This fluid does two things - it preserves the body and restores its natural appearance. As I navigate the arteries with practiced ease, my mind is solely focused on the task at hand - preserving and honoring the life that once flowed through these very vessels.

The embalming fluid courses through the body, seeping into every tissue, halting decay in its tracks. It's a silent partnership between science and reverence for life. With each injection, I am reminded of the weight of my responsibility - to give families a chance to say their final goodbyes in a setting that honors the memory of their loved one.

Once the body is embalmed, the transformation continues. I carefully dress the deceased, selecting garments that speak to their personality and spirit. It's not just about putting clothes on; it's about telling a story. Through their attire, I offer a glimpse into their life - their style, their preferences, their passions.

As I dress the deceased, I find myself getting lost in their story. The fabric slipping through my fingertips becomes a conduit of memories and emotions. It's a humbling experience, a reminder that grief and loss are universal. Each button, each fold becomes a whispered farewell, a delicate acknowledgment of the life that once flourished.

Finally, the time comes for the grand presentation. The deceased is ready to be displayed in a way that allows their loved ones to say goodbye. With the skill of a cosmetic artist, I delicately apply makeup to recreate the natural appearance of life. It's a fine balance - restoring vitality while allowing the individual's essence to shine through.

Now, the deceased rests in a carefully chosen casket adorned with flowers and personal mementos. It's the final act of respect, a precious moment for families to spend with their loved one. As morticians, it's our mission to create an environment of solace and reverence, to offer a space where the grieving can find comfort and closure.

Behind closed doors, funeral homes hold the secrets of morticians. Within these walls, we engage in ancient rituals, meticulously preparing the departed for their final journey. Our task is simple: to honor the life that once graced these halls and to help those left behind find solace and closure.

These secrets, guarded by tradition and respect, are a testament to the care and compassion we pour into our work. We hold these secrets close, serving as silent guardians, making sure that every step of their journey is marked with dignity. Behind closed doors, we create a sanctuary where grief finds solace, love finds expression, and the memories of the deceased are cherished forever.

The Circle of Life: Reflections on Mortality

EVERY DAY, WE COME face to face with a harsh truth: life is fleeting. It's like a blazing firework display in the vastness of time, there and gone in an instant. The bodies that come through our doors serve as powerful reminders of our own mortality, of the inevitable journey we all take back to the earth. But what resonates with me the most is not the finality of death, but rather the incredible journey that leads us there. It's like a rollercoaster ride, full of twists and turns, highs and lows, that forces us to reflect on the importance of every precious moment we're given.

Now, contemplating our own mortality isn't exactly a walk in the park. It forces us to confront the things that scare us most, the vulnerabilities we rather keep hidden. But here's the thing: as morticians, we're thrown into the deep end of death every day. It's a constant presence in our lives. And through this constant exposure, we come to understand the true value of being alive. Every breath we take is a gift, every second spent with our loved ones an opportunity to be cherished. Death, strangely enough, fuels our desire to truly live.

When faced with the fragility of life, we can't help but search for meaning and purpose. We wrestle with the same questions that have bewildered philosophers for centuries: Why are we here? What is the point of our existence? You see, each life that comes through our doors holds its own tale, its own unique experiences. And it's through witnessing these lives that we realize life's meaning doesn't come from grand achievements or hoarding wealth. No, it comes from the connections we make, the impact we have on others. Death forces us to reevaluate our priorities and realize the immense value of love, compassion, and human connection.

In the presence of death, spirituality emerges. Regardless of our beliefs, death unites us all in the understanding that life is a cycle. We're prompted to confront our own notions of what happens after we're gone. Personally, I take comfort in the idea that our spirits continue on, that there's something beyond this physical realm. But regardless of our individual beliefs, what really matters is how we honor and celebrate the lives that have passed through our hands.

You might think that our line of work is morbid, and you wouldn't be wrong. But it offers us a unique perspective on the beauty of existence. It reminds us that life is precious and fleeting, something to be grateful for and marvel at. In the face of death, we find ourselves appreciating the simplest joys life has to offer – the warmth of a loved one's touch, the laughter shared with friends, the awe-inspiring beauty of nature surrounding us.

The circle of life, seen through the eyes of a mortician, is a potent reminder that we're part of something greater than ourselves. It's an incredibly humbling experience that pushes us to cherish the present and be mindful of how we treat others. It compels us to stare our own mortality in the face and think about the path our lives are taking, the legacy we want to leave behind.

Embracing the circle of life, with all its complexity and uncertainty, allows us to fully embrace the human experience. It brings into focus the delicate balance between life and death and underscores the immense significance of every passing moment. As morticians, we're fortunate enough to witness firsthand the profound impact death has on the living. And through this, we're forever changed. We learn to appreciate the fragility and beauty of being alive, finding solace and meaning in both life and death. It's a rare gift that comes from walking alongside death every day, and one that shapes the way we see the world.

Supporting Each Other: A Community of Compassion

The Power of Connection

When I first stepped foot into the world of mortuary work, I envisioned a solitary existence, a one-man show where the only company I'd have would be the deceased. Boy, was I in for a surprise. Turns out, being a mortician is more like being part of a tight-knit crew, a community of individuals who understand death's profound impact on the living and share those experiences firsthand.

I'll never forget the day I realized the power of connection in this profession. It was a particularly tough day, the kind that weighs down your soul with grief and sadness. The families I was serving were drowning in sorrow, and I felt like I was drowning right alongside them. But then, like a flicker of light amidst the dark, my fellow morticians came to my rescue.

During a break in the chaos, we all gathered in the little break room, seeking solace and refuge from the emotional whirlwind outside. And it was there that we began to swap stories, not the triumphant, boastful kind, but the ones that bore our hearts and exposed our vulnerability. We shared the hardships we faced, the swells of emotion that threatened to engulf us, and the toll our work took on our own well-being.

In that moment of raw honesty, a weight was lifted off my shoulders. I realized I wasn't alone in my struggles. There were others who knew the unique challenges of our profession, the toll it could take on our mental and emotional health.

From that day on, I embraced the power of connection. I sought out every opportunity to bond with my fellow morticians, whether it was through professional associations or informal get-togethers. And let me tell you, the value of sharing our stories, our experiences, was immeasurable. It reminded us that we weren't alone, that others carried the same burdens we did, and that together, we were stronger.

In these gatherings, we found a safe space to release our deepest fears and insecurities. We spoke of the haunting moments, the families whose pain etched itself into our hearts, and the unanswerable questions about life and death that plagued our minds. And in the act of sharing, we discovered a collective strength that fortified us against the daily struggles of our work.

But our connection went beyond mere storytelling. In this community, we provided support and understanding in ways that no one else could. We became each other's shoulders to lean on, lending an empathetic ear or offering consoling words when needed. It was as if we were the only ones who truly grasped the weight of our responsibilities, and that understanding forged bonds of connection that were unbreakable.

And let me tell you, the power of connection didn't only come from sharing our stories; it came from the diverse perspectives and insights we gained from one another. We swapped coping mechanisms, experimented with different approaches, and broadened our understanding of how to care for ourselves and our clients. Connection became a wellspring of creativity and growth as we pooled our knowledge and expertise.

In a profession that confronts death and grief on a daily basis, the power of connection acts as a lifeline. It grounds us, reminds us of our purpose, and makes us feel like we belong. It's a constant reminder that we're not alone in our struggles and that the support and understanding of others who tread the same path are incredibly powerful.

So, my dear fellow mortician, I implore you to embrace the power of connection. Seek out your peers, engage in conferences and workshops, and cherish every opportunity to come together as a community. In doing so, you'll find solace, strength, and the invaluable gift of connection that will carry you through this extraordinary journey.

The Healing Circle

WORKING IN THE MORTUARY profession takes a toll on a person, no doubt about it. We're face-to-face with death every single day, witnessing the raw grief of families and friends, and carrying the weight of the deceased's stories on our own shoulders. It's a heavy load to bear, and over time, it can drain us emotionally and leave us feeling completely exhausted and overwhelmed. But here's the thing: as morticians, we've got to take care of ourselves and seek support from others who truly get what we're going through.

That's where the healing circle comes in. It's a safe and nurturing space for morticians just like us to come together, share our experiences, and find solace in knowing that we're not alone. It's a place where we can be understood, where empathy flows freely, and where our feelings are validated. There's something truly magical about the sense of camaraderie that forms within a healing circle. It's like finding a long-lost tribe of people who intimately understand the unique challenges we face every single day.

So, how do you go about creating one of these healing circles? Well, first things first – you need to find like-minded individuals who are also looking to establish a support system. Connect with fellow morticians in your community, whether that's through professional organizations or online forums. Trust me, there are others out there searching for the same kind of support you are. Once you've gathered your crew, the next step is to establish some clear guidelines and boundaries. Safety and respect are key. We want everyone to feel secure in opening up and sharing their vulnerabilities without fear of judgment.

Now, the format of your healing circle can really be whatever works best for your group. You can have guided discussions where you tackle a specific topic or question in each session. This kind of approach helps steer the conversation and allows us to dive deep into our shared experiences. Topics like coping with a particularly difficult case or finding meaning in our work can spark some incredible conversations and lead to personal growth and reflection.

But maybe artsy stuff is more your style. That's totally cool. Engaging in creative activities like painting, writing, or music can be incredibly therapeutic. It's a different way of processing our emotions and letting them out. So, encourage your fellow circle members to express themselves artistically and share their creations with the group. It's a beautiful way to appreciate each other and dive even deeper into our experiences.

Remember, though, that the healing circle is all about listening and empathy. Each person should have the chance to speak their truth without interruption or judgment. Just listening – really listening – can be just as healing as sharing our own stories. It's about validating each other's experiences and emotions, and creating that profound sense of connection and understanding that we all crave.

To keep the healing circle going strong, consistency and commitment are key. Make sure you set regular meeting times and hold each other accountable for showing up and actively participating. That consistency builds trust within the group and provides a reliable space for everyone. And hey, don't be afraid to mix things up if it feels necessary. Ask for feedback, explore new discussion topics, and try out some new creative activities. Keep things fresh and evolving.

While the healing circle is undeniably powerful, it's important to remember that it shouldn't be the only source of support in our lives. We've got to practice individual self-care too. Engage in activities that bring you joy and relaxation, whether that's exercising, meditating, or indulging in your favorite hobbies. Take care of yourself – it's an ongoing process that needs constant attention and effort.

So, my fellow morticians, the healing circle is an incredible tool that we can use to cope with the unique challenges of our profession. It provides us with the emotional release, connection, and personal growth that we desperately need. Through creating and nurturing these circles, and by prioritizing our own self-care, we can find the resilience, healing, and renewed purpose that we need to keep going. Together, we'll support each other through the toughest of times and come out the other side as even stronger, more compassionate morticians.

Building Bridges, Breaking Barriers

YOU KNOW, WHEN IT COMES to building bridges and knocking down barriers, there's something at the core that we can't overlook. It's all about creating a culture of transparency, trust, and inclusivity, my friend. In the world of morticians, they need to feel safe and supported, not just in their professional role but also in their emotional well-being. And that means we gotta create an atmosphere where they can freely share their experiences, seek support, and show their vulnerable side without worrying about being judged or getting in trouble.

You ready to hear some strategies for making that happen? Well, one effective way to cultivate this culture is by opening up communication channels on the regular. Morticians need opportunities to connect with each other, whether it's through meetings, support groups, or even online forums. 'Cause let's face it, this job can sometimes be isolating as hell. By exchanging ideas and experiences, they not only validate each other's struggles but also share coping techniques and resources. It's all about building a community that's strong and resilient, my friend.

But hold up, there's another big hurdle to overcome in this field. The general public has always had a skewed view of morticians, and that's led to a whole lot of stigma and misunderstanding. And you can bet that mess makes it even harder for morticians to open up about what they're going through. It's like a vicious cycle, feeding into secrecy and isolation. We've gotta step up and challenge those stigmas, educate people about the real deal behind this job. If we can demystify the profession and show the crucial support morticians provide to grieving families, we might just see some attitudes shift. Let's create a world that's compassionate and understanding, my friend.

Oh, and let's not forget about mental health. This profession takes a heavy toll on emotions, and if morticians don't address it, they're bound to burn out. We need to strip away the shame and make it clear that it's okay to seek mental health support. I'm talking about employee assistance programs, specifically designed for morticians. These programs should provide access to counseling, support groups, and resources that can help them navigate the emotional rollercoaster of their work.

But it's not just all about EAPs. Morticians need to prioritize self-care and self-compassion too. They need to set boundaries, take care of their well-being. That could mean exercising regularly, practicing mindfulness or meditation, or even finding hobbies that bring them joy outside of the job. It's all about preventing burnout and looking out for number one, my friend.

When we break down these barriers and build bridges within the mortuary community, we're not just helping individual morticians, we're paving the way for positive change in the profession as a whole. By opening up about our challenges, sharing strategies for coping, and supporting one another, we smash those barriers, challenge that stigma, and create a community of compassion and understanding. It's a proactive approach that leads to better mental health for morticians and a stronger profession that can handle anything that comes its way.

So, my friend, it's time to come together, to open our hearts and minds, and to build bridges of understanding in the mortuary community. It's the only way we can create a future that's all about transparency, trust, and inclusivity. A future that puts the well-being of these incredible individuals at the forefront.

Cultivating Compassion

ALRIGHT, FOLKS, BUCKLE up because we're about to dive deep into the world of compassion. We're going to uncover some strategies that can help us cultivate and sustain this beautiful quality in our daily lives. We'll be talking about self-reflection, self-care practices, empathy-building exercises, and mindfulness techniques. Trust me, by the end of this ride, you'll be well-equipped to create a compassionate and caring community for yourself and those around you.

Now, let's start by understanding the importance of self-reflection in cultivating compassion. Take a moment to think about your own experiences, emotions, and reactions. Self-reflection is like peering into a mirror and really seeing yourself. It helps you understand who you are on a deeper level, which makes it easier to empathize with others. Plus, it helps highlight any biases, weaknesses, or triggers you may have. Armed with this knowledge, you can approach every situation with an open heart and an open mind.

Journaling is an amazing self-reflection practice that can work wonders. Just a few minutes each day jotting down your thoughts and emotions can be incredibly liberating. It's like unloading a burden off your chest. Pouring your heart out on paper helps you process your feelings and gain insight into your own experiences. By making journaling a habit, you can develop a better understanding of yourself and how your own emotional landscape affects your interactions with others.

Now, self-reflection is just the tip of the iceberg. We also need to prioritize self-care in our daily routines if we want to sustain compassion. As caretakers, we often put everyone else's needs before our own, forgetting that we can't pour from an empty cup. It's time to put ourselves on the priority list, my friends. Self-care is not selfish; it's necessary for our own well-being and our ability to provide care for others.

Self-care comes in different shapes and sizes, so find what works best for you. Maybe it's sticking to a regular exercise routine or diving into a hobby that brings you pure joy. It could be setting boundaries with work and personal time, or seeking support from therapists or support groups. Whatever it is, remember that taking care of yourself is not a luxury, it's a must.

Let's move on to empathy-building exercises now. Picture this – you can step into someone else's shoes and see the world through their eyes. Sounds pretty powerful, right? That's exactly what empathy-building exercises can do for you. One exercise that works wonders is storytelling. Take the time to really listen to others, to truly hear their experiences. It's like opening a window to their lives and letting the wind of empathy blow in. This exercise nourishes your capacity to connect on a human level and deepens your understanding of others.

Speaking of listening, active listening is a superpower when it comes to showing compassion. When you're having conversations with grieving families, it's critical to be fully present and attentive. Leave your judgments, distractions, and preconceived notions at the door and really listen to what the other person is saying. By doing so, you not only validate their emotions but also create a safe space for them to express their grief.

Now, let's shift our attention to mindfulness techniques. These babies can help us stay in the present moment and cultivate compassion. Mindfulness is all about directing your attention to the here and now without judgment. It allows you to tune in to your own emotions and regulate your responses, saving you from burning out and helping you maintain your compassion.

One mindfulness technique that works wonders is the body scan meditation. Picture yourself lying down in a comfy position and directing your attention to each part of your body. You observe any sensations or tension without passing judgment. This practice helps you ground yourself and can be a real lifesaver when you're feeling stressed or emotionally drained.

To sum it all up, folks, cultivating and sustaining compassion in our daily lives is crucial if we want to effectively support others while preserving our own well-being. Through self-reflection, self-care practices, empathy-building exercises, and mindfulness techniques, we can build our resilience and create a more compassionate and caring community. So let's prioritize compassion and pave the way for a society that understands and empathizes with one another.

Navigating Boundaries

MAINTAINING PROFESSIONAL distance while also offering empathy and support is like walking a tightrope in our line of work. We're constantly thrust into situations filled with grief and loss, comforting families during their darkest hours. It's hard not to feel for the people who are suffering. It's what makes us good at what we do. But we can't let their pain become our own.

I've found that a practical way to navigate this challenge is to remind ourselves that we're here to provide professional care and support, not to get caught up in the emotional whirlwind of others. By recognizing this distinction, we can keep our own emotions in check. It's not about being cold or indifferent; it's about respecting the boundaries between our professional duties and our personal lives. This way, we can offer families the empathy and support they need without sacrificing our own well-being.

Managing the emotional toll of our job is another part of this balancing act that's crucial to get right. Dealing with death and grief day after day can drain us, overwhelming our minds and hearts. That's why it's essential for us to find a balance between staying engaged with our work and taking time for ourselves to decompress.

Personally, I've discovered that establishing a self-care routine is a game-changer. We need to prioritize activities that bring us joy and help us relax. For me, that might mean taking leisurely walks in nature or indulging in creative hobbies like painting or writing. By putting self-care first, we not only protect our mental and emotional well-being, but also ensure we can keep going in this demanding profession. After all, how can we continue to help others if we're not taking care of ourselves?

Finding that balance between being morticians and looking after ourselves can be a tricky tightrope to walk, but it's vital for our long-term sustainability. One way to achieve this balance is by setting clear boundaries around our work hours. It's tempting to always be available for others, but we need to carve out time for rest and rejuvenation.

Creating a routine where we have dedicated time for ourselves, whether it's pursuing our hobbies, spending quality moments with loved ones, or simply taking a breather from work-related responsibilities, allows us to establish a healthy separation between our professional and personal lives. This separation not only recharges us, but also prevents us from being consumed by the demands of our job.

And it's not just about setting boundaries around work hours; it's also about having open and honest communication with our colleagues and supervisors about our needs and limitations. Sometimes, we have to speak up and say no to additional tasks or responsibilities that might overload us. By clearly communicating our boundaries, we ensure that others understand and respect our limitations.

In a profession where the lines between work and personal life can easily blur, it's crucial for our own well-being to establish and maintain healthy boundaries. This not only protects us from the toll our job can take on us, but also allows us to continue offering the empathetic and compassionate care our clients need.

As morticians, we've chosen a line of work that demands incredible strength and resilience. But let's not forget that we're also human beings with our own needs and limitations. By setting clear boundaries, we find the sweet spot between our professional responsibilities and our personal well-being. Navigating boundaries in the mortuary field may be tough, but it's an essential part of self-care. By putting our own well-being first, we can continue providing top-notch care to those who need it most while safeguarding our mental, emotional, and physical health.

Your Ongoing Journey: Embracing Self-Care

Unmasking the Shadows

You know, being in the line of work that we're in, we're constantly face-to-face with death. It's no walk in the park, let me tell you. Every single day, we're hit with grief, loss, and the cold, hard truth of mortality. It's enough to make even the toughest of us feel overwhelmed, you know?

But here's the thing, there's another heavy emotion that us morticians often deal with that not a lot of people talk about - compassion fatigue. It's like this emotional exhaustion that comes from being around so much pain for so long. We're the ones who have to comfort and support families in their darkest moments. We're like their rock, helping them get through it all. But somehow, in the process, we forget to take care of ourselves.

I remember this one time that really opened my eyes to what compassion fatigue can do. There was a mother who had just lost her young daughter in a terrible accident. She was devastated, and I was standing right by her side, listening to the heart-wrenching cries. And let me tell you, in that moment, I felt like her grief seeped into my soul. It left me drained and emotionally wiped out. It was like I was carrying her pain on my own shoulders.

By sharing stories like this, my hope is to shine a light on some of the struggles we face in our profession. We need to recognize that we're not superheroes, we're human beings who feel things deeply. It's only natural for us to be affected by the suffering we see.

It's not an easy thing to unmask these shadows. It takes a lot of courage to dig deep into our own vulnerabilities and confront our own emotions. But it's necessary for our own healing and growth.

You know, after all these years, I've come to realize that self-care is not a privilege, it's an absolute necessity. It's like the oxygen mask on a plane - we have to take care of ourselves first before we can help others. If we're running on empty, we're no good to anyone. So, self-care has to be a priority if we want to keep providing that compassionate care to those who need it.

In my own journey of unmasking the shadows, I've found some helpful coping mechanisms. One thing that's really been valuable for me is journaling. There's something about putting pen to paper and giving a voice to the emotions weighing on my heart. It's like a release, a way to find comfort in the written word.

And let me tell you, seeking support from people who truly understand is a game-changer. Being able to lean on a network of empathetic individuals who get it, who can provide a safe space for us to express ourselves, it's invaluable. Whether it's through support groups, therapy, or just opening up to a trusted friend, sharing the burden can make a world of difference.

We also need to show ourselves some compassion, my friend. It's so much easier to be kind to others than it is to be kind to ourselves. But embracing self-compassion reminds us that we deserve the same level of care and tenderness that we give to others. It's a gentle nudge to look after ourselves, to nurture our own souls.

And we can't forget the importance of finding balance in our lives. This profession can consume us if we let it. So we have to make time for self-care, for hobbies, for things that bring us joy. Taking care of our own interests and passions helps bring a sense of equilibrium back into our lives and helps us avoid burning ourselves out.

In the end, unmasking the shadows is a personal journey, a transformation of the heart and soul. It's not an easy road to travel, my friend. It requires bravery, vulnerability, and a willingness to confront the dark side of our profession and ourselves. But by shedding light on these hidden emotions and vulnerabilities, we learn more about who we are. We find ways to cope and heal. And through this journey of self-discovery, we become stronger, more compassionate, and better equipped to continue serving those in need.

The Dance of Life and Death

AS A MORTICIAN, I'VE seen some truly incredible things. You see, we have a unique perspective on the transition from life to death. We witness the delicate dance between the two, as one fades away and the other embarks on its eternal journey. It's a dance that'll leave you in awe and remind you of just how fragile and impermanent life really is.

In my years of serving as a mortician, I've come to understand that death is not just the end. No, it's more like a gateway to something new, something different. It's a profound transformation, a transition from the physical to the spiritual. And it's our job as morticians to guide and support individuals and their loved ones through this intricate process.

To truly grasp this dance, you have to appreciate the beauty and fragility of life itself. Life is like a tapestry, woven with threads of joy and sorrow, love and loss. It's the moments of true happiness and connection that make us realize just how precious our existence really is. And when death stares us in the face, it's a cruel reminder to savor every breath we take.

You know, when I first started out as a mortician, death hit me hard. The grief surrounding me was suffocating, and it started to wear me down. It was like I was drowning in sadness. But then, I shifted my perspective. Instead of being consumed by the darkness, I started to look for the bright spots. The moments of joy and celebration that mingled in with the sorrow.

One memory, above all others, forever changed my outlook on death. It was the funeral of a young woman who had lost her battle with cancer. The sorrow surrounding her was palpable as her family gathered around her casket. But as the service went on, something incredible happened. Amongst the tears and pain, there were moments of laughter and joy. Loved ones shared stories of her vibrant spirit, her love for life, and the impact she had on those around her.

In that moment, I saw life and death intertwine like a graceful dance. Death wasn't this dark shroud, but more like a gentle breeze carrying her spirit into eternity. It reminded me that even in the face of death, life continued to flourish in the hearts of those left behind. And it became my solemn duty to preserve those memories, honor the life that was lived, and guide those grieving on their healing journey.

This dance requires us to embrace the ebb and flow of life and death. We have to accept that death is a natural part of our human experience. But it's not the end. No, it's a transition, a sacred passage that allows the departed souls to continue their journey beyond this physical realm. And in understanding this, we find solace and purpose in our profession.

But make no mistake, navigating this dance can be challenging. We morticians face our own mortality on a daily basis. The transient nature of life is always lingering in the back of our minds. And witnessing the grief and pain of families can sometimes weigh heavy on our hearts. That's when compassion fatigue becomes our constant companion, threatening to consume our own well-being.

Yet, even in the darkest moments, there's a glimmer of hope. We have the power to transform our own experiences and find healing within this dance. Taking care of ourselves becomes crucial. We must acknowledge our own vulnerability and the impact death has on our psyche. Processing our emotions, seeking support from peers and loved ones, and engaging in activities that bring us joy and fulfillment become essential to finding the balance we need to keep serving others.

In the end, the dance of life and death is a profound tapestry, and we morticians are privileged to be a part of it. It reminds us of the fragility and impermanence of life, but it also highlights the incredible beauty and resilience that exists within each individual. So, we embrace this dance, understanding the sacredness of death and the preciousness of life. And through it all, we navigate the challenges of our profession with compassion, grace, and resilience. Because in doing so, we not only honor those we serve, but also nurture our own well-being. The dance keeps on going, and we are the ones who keep its rhythm.

Embracing Vulnerability

YOU KNOW, VULNERABILITY gets a bad rap sometimes. We're taught to believe that it's a sign of weakness or something to be ashamed of. But let me tell you, as morticians, we're no strangers to vulnerability. We see it every day in our line of work, how fragile and impermanent life can be. We're there for the deceased and their loved ones, witnessing firsthand the vulnerable state of human existence.

And it's high time we started recognizing the strength that comes with embracing our own vulnerability.

Now, hold on a minute. I'm not saying we should all turn into blubbering messes or spill our deepest secrets to everyone we meet. Embracing vulnerability is about being authentic, allowing ourselves to be seen and heard. It's about creating a safe space where our clients and colleagues feel comfortable sharing their own vulnerabilities. When we can accept and honor our own vulnerability, we open the door for others to do the same.

But let me tell you, it's not always easy. Managing our own emotions is a big part of embracing vulnerability. It's easy to become desensitized to the pain and grief around us, but bottling up our emotions only leads to burnout and compassion fatigue. We have to acknowledge and process our feelings, and sometimes that means seeking support from trusted friends, family, or therapists who can guide us through the emotional turmoil that comes with our work.

And speaking of turmoil, grief and loss are messy and uncomfortable. We have to become comfortable with uncertainty and sit with our own discomfort. It's not always easy, but being present for others' pain is part of our job. We have to develop emotional agility, where we can navigate those difficult emotions without shutting down. That's how healing and growth happen.

Now, if we're being real here, we also need to confront our own fears and insecurities. Fear of judgment or rejection can hold us back from showing our true selves. We worry that being vulnerable makes us weak or incapable. But let me tell you something: vulnerability is not weakness. It takes a hell of a lot of strength and resilience to be vulnerable. When we face our fears head-on and challenge the stories that hold us back, we open ourselves up to incredible growth and connection.

And guess what? Embracing vulnerability doesn't just benefit us personally. It has a profound impact on our professional lives as morticians. When we let vulnerability into our work, we become more in tune with our clients' needs and emotions. We're better able to offer genuine empathy and support, creating a safe space for grieving families to heal. By embracing our own vulnerability, we show others that it's okay to express their emotions and seek support.

So, how do we embrace vulnerability in a practical way? Well, it starts with self-compassion. We have to treat ourselves kindly and understand that we all have struggles. Self-compassion creates an environment that fosters vulnerability and growth. And let's not forget about gratitude. It's important to focus on the positive aspects of our work and be thankful for the lives we honor and support. Gratitude helps us maintain a resilient and open mindset.

In the end, vulnerability is not something to be ashamed of. It's a strength that allows us to connect deeply with ourselves and our clients. By redefining how we see vulnerability and adopting practical strategies for embracing it, we can cultivate a more compassionate and resilient approach to our work as morticians.

The Art of Self-Compassion

YOU KNOW, BEING A MORTICIAN is no easy gig. Every day, we're surrounded by death and grief, and it can really take a toll on our hearts and minds. We're expected to be these pillars of strength for the families we serve, but sometimes, we're left with little room to process our own emotions. It's like we have this invisible weight on our shoulders, carrying the pain of others without taking the time to acknowledge our own. But here's the thing – we need to show ourselves the same compassion we show everyone else. It's not just for our personal well-being, it's for the quality of care we can offer.

You see, self-compassion starts with recognizing that we're only human. We're bound to feel pain and vulnerability, just like anyone else. So instead of beating ourselves up or judging our own suffering, we need to embrace it with kindness and empathy. It's not about brushing off the pain we witness or experience, it's about facing it head-on and offering ourselves the support we need.

One way to cultivate self-compassion in the midst of this challenging work is through self-reflective journaling. Just take a few moments each day to sit quietly and reflect on your experiences. Be real with yourself, no judgment or analysis allowed. Let your feelings flow onto the page. It's like giving those unacknowledged emotions a chance to breathe, and it opens the door for self-compassion to grow.

Another tool in our arsenal is mindfulness meditation. Find a quiet spot, get comfy, and focus on your breath for a little while. When thoughts pop up, don't beat yourself up about it – just acknowledge them and gently bring your attention back to your breath. This practice helps us be kinder to ourselves as we navigate the emotional demands of our profession.

Now, let's talk about self-care. It's not some fancy indulgence or selfish act. It's a downright necessity for maintaining our emotional well-being. Find what brings you joy and make it a priority in your life. Take a walk in nature, lose yourself in a good book, or treat yourself to a well-deserved bath. These activities aren't luxuries; they're life-lines that keep us going.

And let's not forget about setting boundaries. It's okay to say no when we're feeling overwhelmed or in need of some alone time. We need to protect our well-being, both in our personal and professional lives. By establishing clear limits, we give ourselves the power to prioritize what's most important – and that's taking care of ourselves, so we can keep offering compassionate care to others.

Speaking of support, let's nurture our relationships with fellow morticians who know the struggles we face. Seek out professional networks or support groups where you can share your experiences, seek guidance, and feel that sense of belonging. Sometimes, just knowing we're not alone in this journey can be immensely healing.

Now, remember – self-compassion is not a one-time thing. It's a lifelong practice that takes time, patience, and commitment. There will be moments when we feel overwhelmed or drained, and that's when we need to remind ourselves that we deserve the same compassion we extend to others. Self-compassion is our anchor in the storms of stress and compassion fatigue. It's what helps us bounce back, find resilience, and feel deeply fulfilled in our noble profession.

In the chapters to come, we'll dive deeper into self-care practices, coping strategies for compassion fatigue, and ways to maintain our emotional well-being. By engaging in the art of self-compassion, we crack open the door to healing and personal growth. And that, my friends, allows us to continue serving our community with empathy, grace, and unwavering strength.

Finding Light in the Darkness

LET ME TELL YOU ABOUT the incredible stories of hope and transformation that I have come across in my career. These stories, amidst all the pain and sorrow, have managed to find light in the darkest corners of people's lives. They serve as beacons of hope, casting rays of warmth in the midst of sorrow.

One haunting case that will stay with me forever is about a young couple who had tragically lost their son in an accident.

When they arrived at the funeral home, their hearts were heavy with grief, and their pain was visible in their hollow eyes. As I walked them through the funeral planning process, I listened intently to their stories and memories of their precious son. And amidst their tears, I saw a flicker of light.

They shared stories of their son's infectious laughter and joy that could light up any room. They spoke about his dreams, aspirations, and the love he had for everyone around him. As I pieced together the fragments of their son's life, I realized the incredible strength that resided within this young couple. They were determined to honor their son's memory and celebrate the brightness he had brought into their lives.

Together, we crafted a funeral service that truly celebrated their son's spirit. Amidst the grief-stricken crowd, there was a sense of love and unity. The couple had chosen to embrace the light within their darkness, providing solace and comfort to themselves and those around them.

Stories like these exemplify the power of finding light amidst darkness. As morticians, we have the privilege of witnessing these transformations and the resilience of the human spirit. We can learn from these stories, internalize their profound lessons, and apply them in our own lives.

Another story that deeply impacted me was that of an elderly widow who had lost her husband of sixty years. When she arrived at the funeral home, she seemed devoid of life, her eyes glazed over with grief. Her every breath felt like a cry for the void she felt without her partner by her side. But as she reminisced about the life she had shared with her husband, I noticed glimpses of happiness. Their love was unbreakable, transcending time. Instead of drowning in sorrow, she chose to celebrate their love and the life they had created together.

The funeral became a poignant celebration of a well-lived life and a love that defied all odds. Through tears, laughter, and heartfelt stories, family and friends came together to remember a man who had left an indelible mark on their lives. The widow emerged from this experience with a renewed sense of purpose, determined to carry on her husband's legacy of love and kindness.

These stories of resilience and transformation highlight the power of finding light in the darkest moments. They remind us that no matter how deep the grief and despair, there is always a glimmer of hope waiting to be discovered. It is up to us, both as morticians and as individuals, to seek out that light, embrace it, and let it guide us towards healing and inner peace.

I have shared just a few of the countless stories I have encountered throughout my career, each serving as a testament to the strength and resilience of the human spirit. By learning from these narratives and incorporating their lessons into our own lives, we can cultivate compassion, resilience, and self-care.

Finding light in the darkness is not a one-time endeavor but a lifelong practice. It requires us to actively seek out moments of brightness amidst the sorrow and pain. It encourages us to celebrate the memories and legacies of those we have lost, cherishing the light they brought into our lives.

As morticians, we are privileged to witness the profound impact that finding light in the darkness can have on our own well-being. It allows us to navigate the challenges of our profession with resilience and grace. By sharing these stories of hope and transformation, I hope to inspire fellow morticians to embrace the power of light and recognize its potential to heal ourselves and others.

So, as we continue on this journey of self-care and compassion, let us remember that even in the darkest of times, there is always light to be found. Through the stories of the resilient souls we have encountered, we can discover the strength within ourselves to navigate the trials and tribulations of our profession. Let us strive to shine our light, both for ourselves and for the families we serve, in order to create a brighter, more compassionate world.

About the Author

Elena Blackwood was born into a family deeply rooted in the mortuary profession, inheriting not only a legacy but also a profound understanding of the delicate art of caring for the departed. Growing up surrounded by the solemn yet compassionate atmosphere of her parents' funeral home, Elena developed a unique perspective on life, death, and the importance of self-care amidst the solemnity of her chosen profession.

Following in her parents' footsteps, Elena pursued her education in mortuary science with unwavering dedication and a thirst for knowledge. Armed with both traditional wisdom and modern techniques, she honed her skills as a mortician, mastering the intricacies of embalming, restorative art, and funeral arrangement.

However, it was through her intimate connection with death that Elena discovered the paramount importance of self-care, not only for the bereaved but also for those who serve them. Drawing from her own experiences and the wisdom passed down through generations, she embarked on a journey to redefine self-care within the mortuary profession.

Elena Blackwood's passion for holistic well-being led her to explore various modalities, from mindfulness practices to physical exercises tailored to alleviate the unique challenges faced by morticians. With empathy as her guiding light, she became an advocate for self-compassion and resilience, championing the notion that caring for oneself is not only essential but also a profound act of reverence for the departed.

Today, Elena Blackwood stands as a beacon of compassion and understanding in the mortuary community, offering solace to both the living and the deceased. Through her tireless dedication to the art of mortuary care and her unwavering commitment to self-care, she continues to inspire others to embrace the beauty of life, even in the face of death.